THE EVOLVING

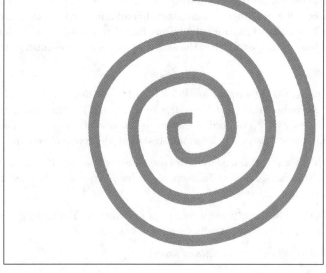

MULTICULTURAL
CLASSROOM

ROSE REISSMAN

Association for Supervision and Curriculum Development
Alexandria, Virginia

About the Author

Rose Reissman is a curriculum writer, workshop leader, and Impact II educator in the New York City Public Schools. She is President of the New York City Association of Teachers of English and Vice President of the Association of Computer Educators. In addition, she is a field editor for *Learning Magazine* and serves on *New York Newsday*'s Educational Advisory Board. She teaches at Manhattanville College and Fordham University. Address correspondence to the author at 110 Seaman Avenue, Apt. 5C, New York, NY 10034.

Association for Supervision and Curriculum Development, 1250 N. Pitt Street, Alexandria, VA 22314-1453
Telephone: (703) 549-9110   Fax: (703) 549-3891

Ronald S. Brandt, *Executive Editor*
Nancy Modrak, *Managing Editor, Books*
Carolyn R. Pool, *Associate Editor*
Biz McMahon, *Assistant Editor*
Gary Bloom, *Manager, Design and Production Services*
Stephanie A. Justen, *Print Production Coordinator*
Valerie Sprague, *Desktop Publisher*

Price: $13.95
ASCD Stock No.: 1-94173

Library of Congress Cataloging-in-Publication Data

Reissman, Rose.
    The evolving multicultural classroom/ Rose Reissman.
      p. cm.
    Includes bibliographical references and index.
    "ASCD stock no.: 1-94173"—T.p. verso.
    ISBN 0-87120-233-6 : $13.95
    1. Multicultural education—United States—Handbooks, manuals,
etc. 2. Multicultural education—United States—Curricula.
3. Multicultural education—United States—Activity programs.
I. Title.
LC1099.3.R45   1994
370.19'6'973—dc20
                                                 94-25103
                                                   CIP

The Evolving Multicultural Classroom

This book is dedicated to my mother, Sidonia ("Simi") Blank Reissman.
Her cultural commitment, energies, knowledge, creativity,
and passion inspired the multicultural activities of this book.

Introduction

Multicultural education . . . is about all
people; it is also *for* all people.
                Sonio Nieto, *Affirming Diversity*
                        (1992, p. 213)

Multicultural education deals with all
Americans, all their struggles, hopes, and
dreams. . . . Multicultural education is
for everybody.
                James A. Banks, *Teaching Tolerance*
                        (1992, p. 21)

It [multicultural education] should not
be an add-on. Multicultural education
should be an integral part of what we do.
. . . We teach the same areas; we may reconceptualize them, but it's not something added on.
                James A. Banks, *Teaching Tolerance*
                        (1992, p. 22)

Everybody has a culture, whether clearly
manifested in its more traditional forms
or not.
                Sonia Nieto, *Affirming Diversity*
                        (1992, p. 16)

Although we almost all have an immi-
grant past, very few of us know or even
acknowledge it.
                Sonia Nieto, *Affirming Diversity*
                        (1992, p. xxv)

I have been a classroom language arts/so-
cial studies educator for more than twenty
years and a teacher educator for about ten of
those years. I've been exposed to, "trained in,"
and "district" *initiated* into a seemingly never-
ending stream of educational movements. The
buzzwords for various educational seasons included collaborative learning, global learning,
cooperative learning, inquiry-based approaches, assessment, student-centered learning, integrated language arts, whole language,
critical thinking, writing across the curriculum, community service learning, right brain
learning, and multiple intelligences theory.
Some of these movements proved to be transi-
tory educational fashions, much like the fashion world's mini or grunge looks; others
continually resurfaced, sometimes under different names or theorist's banners. The ones that
continually reappeared, such as community living, now called "real life" skills or "intergroup
respect," articulated the core elements of good
teaching. These particular educational buzzwords or "in" movements were really just re-
namings or linguistic taggings of aspects of
teaching that were integral to the mission of all
classroom teachers. *This mission is to assist students at all grade levels in acquiring sufficient
processes, information, self-knowledge, and self-
concept to become proactive, committed participants in their communities and on the world
scene.*

Through all my training sessions for the
burgeoning numbers of educational movements and my study of their rationales, I listened for the common chord to strike within
my own culture of teaching. When I recognized
theoretical principles that made a concrete connection to my own experiences, I integrated the
precepts of the movement into my teaching—
not only for the year or two it was fashionable,
but beyond. Only a few movements of the past

1

two decades have elicited that recognition or "chord" of identification from me. But multicultural education, one fairly new movement gaining momentum across the United States, though generating controversy, has struck that chord of recognition. The movement is so highly charged that even its name shifts in various locations. To reduce the sting of controversy engendered by multiculturalism, it is also known as "cultural diversity," "diversity training," "intergroup dynamics," "ethnic studies," and a host of other labels. By any other name, multicultural education is a process I have found to be an integral part of my evolved teaching philosophies and methodologies.

But stop right there—I sense both veteran teachers and new teachers shifting uneasily in their seats—even if this is the most relevant contributing movement to education since John Dewey's philosophies. You may be protesting: "My plan book and my curriculums are full to the brim with state and federal mandates, as well as district initiatives. I can't get training in any more theories and methodologies. There's no place to add this movement into my course."

Multicultural education is not another theory and methodology or add-on burden to be tagged on to teachers' already overweighted district, state, and federal top-down agendas. Although infusing multicultural awareness across the curriculum requires grounding in theories articulated by key researchers, such studies make teachers aware that the key tenets of multiculturalism are synonymous with good teaching practice. Most teachers strive to foster intergroup understanding, equity, excellence in subject mastery, student knowledge and respect for others' cultures, education for social justice,

antiracist education, and the development of proactive community, national, and global citizenship. These teachers are already participating in the *process* of infusing multicultural understanding. Understanding—and *highlighting*—multicultural methodologies and theories assists teachers, students, and parents in the very activities that most people consider important in education. In the process, teachers become metacognitive about the extent to which multiculturalism permeates their teaching.

Metacognitive? Isn't this much too abstract? You may be asking, "Wait a minute. In what ways did you, a veteran English and social studies teacher, come to realize that you were teaching 'multiculturally' as an integral part of your daily routine?"

When I teach literature, I always approach it by having students analyze the commonality in experiences, as well as the specific cultural events or characteristics that inspired the work. In teaching any literary work, I train the students to explore through multiple perspectives. I share my own ethnic sensibilities as a catalyst to inviting students to examine theirs. I encourage students to explore, examine, and articulate their own diverse backgrounds through oral histories, interviews with their families, and research. But I also encourage them to appreciate the cultures and concerns of others through panel discussions, examination of news from multiple perspectives, and more research. Students create their own "Bills of Responsibility" and social-community service and rights initiatives to help them evolve concepts of social justice. They network proactively in their school, city, and national community.

Teacher to Teacher

I hope that as you read this book, you will be saying:

Now I'm beginning to get it. If multiculturalism is a process of preparing students for meaningful participation in a diverse world and for assisting them in affirming their own unique cultural backgrounds while respecting others', then of course I am "doing it" already. How can I begin to highlight the inherently multicultural aspects of my own teaching so that my students, their parents, and I can become an advocate for "metacognitive" multicultural education?

In framing the question, you've already begun the process. Now it's time to get some grounding in the ideas of the two theorists—liberally quoted at the beginning of this Introduction—whose principles of multicultural education articulate the ways this process inherently infuses effective teaching.

References

Banks, J.A. (Fall 1992). "It's Up to Us." (Interview). *Teaching Tolerance*, pp. 20–23.

Nieto, S. (1992). *Affirming Diversity: The Sociopolitical Context of Multicultural Education*. White Plains, N.Y.: Longman.

SECTION 1

ENGAGEMENT

1 Definitions of Multicultural Education

The goal of multicultural education is an education for freedom. . . . Multicultural education should help students to develop the knowledge, attitudes, and skills to participate in a democratic and free society. . . . Multicultural education promotes the freedom, abilities and skills to cross ethnic and cultural boundaries to participation in other cultures and groups.

> James A. Banks, *Focus in Change*
> (quoted in Lockwood 1992, p. 23)

Multicultural education is an education for freedom . . . that is essential in to-day's ethnically polarized and troubled world.

> James A. Banks,
> *Educational Leadership*
> (1991/1992, p. 32)

To fully participate in our democratic society, these students and all students need the skills a multicultural education can give them to understand others and to thrive in a rapidly changing, diverse world.

> James A. Banks,
> *Teaching Strategies for Ethnic Studies*
> (1991, p. 35)

Two theorists who have been influential in my development of multicultural education strategies are James A. Banks and Sonia Nieto.

James A. Banks— Education for Freedom

The primary theorist in multicultural education is James Banks, who is Professor of Education and Director of the Center for Multicultural Education at the University of Washington, Seattle. He is a past president of the National Council for the Social Studies and has written or edited fourteen books on multicultural education.

Banks conceives of multicultural education as "education for freedom" and as "an inclusive and cementing movement" (quoted in Lockwood 1992, pp. 23, 27). He has articulated three essential goals of multicultural education.

1. *Multicultural education helps students realize both academic excellence and cultural excellence.* Banks defines "cultural excellence" in terms of students' knowledge of their own cultural backgrounds and initiation in the studies of the differing cultural backgrounds of their peers (Lockwood 1992). As part of this cultural self-knowledge, students develop the skills to express and act on the answers to the following questions: Who am I? Where have I been? What do I hope to do? The answers to these questions—or at least reflections on them—help students function in their own world, as well as in the larger community.

2. *Multicultural education nurtures students' hearts, as well as their minds, in school.*

3. *The multicultural education process helps students develop positive cultural, national, and*

global identification. By *cultural identification*, Banks means students' identification with church, neighborhood, community, and school. *National identification* connotes students' ability to live competently and function positively as citizens in their society. Through *global identification*, students develop an understanding of how their own lives play a part in the whole world picture.

Banks visualizes these goals being infused into the curriculum by teachers who receive training in skills for teaching ethnic content and working with an increasingly diverse multicultural population. He conceives of the training as a way that teachers can examine their own cultural history and ethnic journey. He states, "Once teachers connect to their own cultural experience, it will be a vehicle enabling them to relate to the culture of the kids" (Lockwood 1992, p. 26). If teachers are to incorporate multicultural education process training into their daily teaching, Banks believes that they themselves must experience what he calls "paradigm shifts."

A *paradigm shift* is a change of perspective on subject content and instructional authority. As Banks states, "The teacher needs to understand the nature of knowledge and to understand that knowledge is a process" (quoted in Lockwood 1992, p. 26). Banks focuses on teachers assisting students in raising questions so they can investigate the perspectives of different cultural groups. He also notes that inherently no teacher (or student), however knowledgeable, can know all the answers.

To implement the process of multicultural curriculum reform, Banks (1988; see also Banks and Banks 1991) has outlined four successive levels of integration of ethnic content. These levels are called *approaches*. They provide teachers with an easily infusible, curriculum-stepladder entry into the ongoing process of multicultural education.

Level 1. The Contributions Approach

The Level 1 approach highlights cultural heroes, holidays, and discrete cultural elements. For example, the language arts teacher can focus on specific cultural holidays and heroes. Students could read stories or myths and then retell, report, and reflect on these heroes' contributions to community, national, and global culture. As part of the social studies curriculums, students could study biographies of specific cultural heroes. They could investigate the traditions and historical contexts of various cultural holidays. On a secondary level, language arts students could analyze specific cultural literary styles and dialects (e.g., the *haiku* genre of poetry). Secondary social studies students could analyze specific cultural practices and their consequences for those individuals' social and economic lives.

Level 2. The Additive Approach

At Level 2, the classroom time spent on multicultural investigations is greatly expanded with literal "add on" units dealing in depth with content, concepts, themes, and perspectives. On Level 1, Native American heroes' mythology might only have been represented by a single story detailing Native American *contributions* to mythology. On Level 2, however, the teacher would set aside a block of time to study several myths. On Level 1, students would have the option of reading biographies that documented the contributions of various Latino subgroup members to global culture; but as part of Level 2, the teacher would add a unit of class study devoted to the contributions of the Latinos to global culture—without changing the curriculum. In an additive approach to the integration of ethnic content, units of study are added on to the existing curriculum *without transforming the methodologies and structure of that curriculum*.

Level 3. The Transformation Approach

Level 3 of Banks' metaphoric stepladder involves altering the structure of the set curriculum to enable students to view concepts, issues, events, and themes from diverse ethnic and cultural perspectives. How is this approach different from the contribution and additive approaches to multicultural education? In the Native American mythology example, rather than looking at isolated myths or adding a unit of study on Native American myths, teachers and students using a Level 3 approach would develop a new unit of comparative mythology study analyzing common themes, as well as unique cultural tales. This unit would be developed, piloted, and shaped by student responses. In the social studies content area, teachers would not be limited to examining one specific Puerto Rican festival, for example, or spending a period or two studying Puerto Rican holidays and festivals. Rather, on Level 3, teachers and students would restructure the curriculum with a new unit or module focusing on Puerto Rican holidays and festivals, including those of the native Puerto Ricans themselves, New Yorkers of Puerto Rican extraction, Cubans, Caucasian Americans, Black Americans, Spaniards, and other cultural groups.

The key distinctions between Banks' Levels 1 and 2, and Level 3 is that, on the transformational level, the teacher literally "pulls out," "redesigns," and "creates anew" the existing curriculum. Picture the concrete representations of the existing curriculum structure—lesson plans, handouts, texts, visuals—being tossed into a wastepaper basket or (if kept) realigned, refocused, and submerged into a new array of texts, handouts, and approaches. The original structure, unit, or module of activities has been restructured or transformed so that students are engaged in *exploring the content through multiple perspectives of diverse ethnic and cultural groups*.

Level 4. Social Action Approach

Banks' Level 4 approach enhances student engagement in exploring multiple perspectives by having them make decisions on issues and take actions to solve them. The key focus words for this approach are *social* and *action*. In activities at this level, students and teachers reach out to families, colleagues, and community members. They work collaboratively on projects that can range from a desktop-published *Parent and Child Book of Cultural Heroes*, letters of protest to a local newspaper about the biased coverage of a particular cultural group, community-financed and -coordinated multilingual greeting cards, and student lobbying for a special needs legislative bill.

Banks does not expect teachers to immediately integrate ethnic content on Levels 3 and 4, although these approaches are the desirable ones that can best facilitate "education for freedom" and make the multicultural education process "an inclusive and cementing one." Rather, by using the various approaches and stepladder gradations, teachers can assess their own growth, as well as the multicultural education programs in their classrooms.

Common Misconceptions About Multicultural Education

Finally, it is important to consider Banks' comments on many of the mistakenly controversial, combative aspects of multiculturalism ascribed to this educational process by parents, the general public, administrators, and teaching colleagues not sufficiently grounded in academically accepted multicultural education theories. Banks' theories address many of the objections to the integration of multiethnic understandings across the curriculum and should be used by teachers to back up their practices in the face of potential misconceptions.

Among the commonly misunderstood perceptions of multiculturalism Banks explicates are:

• **_Misconception 1_**. _Multicultural education is education for and about minorities and persons of color. It is not relevant to Caucasian teachers and students. Further, multicultural education should by its nature be taught by persons of color._

Banks has responded to this widely held, inaccurate assessment of multicultural education by noting:

> We talk about kids who are at risk, but . . . we are all at risk if we don't create a society that is united.
>
> Banks (1992, p. 23)

> Multicultural education is for all children, not just for African Americans or Hispanics or Native Americans, but for all students.
>
> Banks (quoted in Lockwood 1992, p. 3)

As Banks explicitly states: "Another misconception is that teachers who are not minorities cannot teach multicultural education" (1992, p. 23). The author of this book and the body of initial curriculums, practices, projects, and workshops it grew out of, is a Caucasian Jewish female from Brooklyn. Enough said.

Banks also notes that "multicultural education deals with all Americans, all of their struggles, hopes and dreams, including white America" (1992, p. 21).

• **_Misconception 2_**. _Like countless other buzzwords and dated educational "fashions of the times," multicultural education is another "add on" to an already overburdened, unrealistic teaching load of standards and goals._

Banks responds that multicultural education is "not an add on. We teach the same areas, we may reconceptualize them, but it's not something added on. Remember the Add on Approach is only step 2 in a ladder of 4 approaches" (1992, p. 22).

• **_Misconception 3_**. _Multicultural education should be limited to those inner cities with increasingly diverse populations._

Banks reminds us of the broader mission of multicultural education. He conceives of it as

> a reform movement designed to bring about educational equity for all students . . . to create a school environment that is equitable and just. Multiculturalism ultimately is a way of thinking: It's recognizing other perspectives, but it's more than recognition. It's caring, and taking action to make our society more just and humane." (1992, p. 21)

Sonia Nieto—Cultural Equity

Sonia Nieto, who is Program Director of the Cultural Diversity and Curriculum Reform Program, School of Education, University of Massachusetts-Amherst, echoes much of Banks' theories of multicultural education as an inclusive, questioning process for cultural equity.

She identifies seven basic characteristics of multicultural education. They are formulated as "endings" to the affirmative statement—

> Multicultural education is
> . . . antiracist education
> . . . basic education
> . . . important for all students
> . . . pervasive
> . . . education for social justice
> . . . a process
> . . . critical pedagogy (1992, p. 208).

Whereas Banks' emphasis in furthering multicultural education is in staff development and curriculum integration, Nieto's key work _Affirming Diversity: The Sociopolitical Context of Multicultural Education_ (1992) explores how personal, social, political, and educational factors have interacted to affect the success of multiethnic students. She details the educational impact of discrimination, racism, school policies, social/economic class, ethnicity, teacher preparation, teacher expectations, and language.

Teachers of language arts and social studies, in particular, can absorb considerable insights into the key role of language as a tool for multicultural education. Nieto notes: "Language is particularly important in multicultural education for it describes and defines people of many groups." She suggests two key questions teachers should frame as they establish their own ongoing class dialogues with multiethnic students. They are: What ethnic/cultural classification (e.g., Latino, Cuban, Jewish American, Black, Afro-American, etc.) do the individuals in question want to be called? What is the most precise term? (1992).

The centerpiece of Nieto's theory is the primacy of

> language choices . . . to *affirm* diversity . . . . Language can capture only imperfectly the nuances of who we are as people. But language, like multicultural education itself, is a process that is in constant flux. We therefore need to pay close attention to the connotations and innuendoes of its daily use (1992, p. 101).

℀   ℀   ℀

This chapter began as a partial response to teachers' needs to be grounded in the underlying theories, approaches, and ideologies of the multicultural education process. Many volumes can and have been written exploring the rationale, principles, and broad implementation of multicultural education theories. The purpose of this book, however, is to provide teachers with a metaphoric highlighter—and concrete strategies—that will enhance the multicultural components of current language arts, social studies, and arts curriculums—as well as integrated curriculums. As you infuse multicultural understandings into your classroom, I hope you will continue to read theories by key researchers to inform your practice and to provide support in face of potential controversies that can rise out of public misconceptions about multicultural education. Figure 1.1 provides several tenets of multicultural education published by the National Education Policy

Network of the National School Boards Association (Mack 1992); and Figure 1.2 provides definitions of multicultural education culled from interviews with James Banks. The tenets and definitions in these figures can be used to inform parent, teacher, and community groups about the process of evolving a multicultural classroom. These definitions can also assist in the encouragement of community feedback and evaluation, which is an essential part of the assessment of student work.

FIGURE 1.1

Tenets of Multicultural Education

Carl Mack, Jr., superintendent of the Del Rosa Heights School District in Sacramento, California, emphasizes six tenets of multicultural education. First:

[Multicultural education] must improve the educational performance of every student.
Carl Mack, Jr.,
Updating School Board Policies (1992, p. 1)

Mack quotes Corey Cook (*The Davis Enterprise*, May 5, 1992) for the other five tenets of multicultural education:

- Multicultural education should offer a diversified curriculum that presents the views and perspectives of many peoples.

- It should be based on the assumption that there is no single correct interpretation of history.

- Curriculum achieves relevance by stressing comparative analysis through different cultural viewpoints.

- [Multicultural education] must hold at its core the principle of eradicating racial/cultural/religious stereotypes.

- Multicultural education presents a balance between understanding cultural similarities and differences and encouraging individuals to maintain and broaden their own cultures and cultural perspectives.
Coney Cooke (quoted in Mack 1992, p. 1)

FIGURE 1.2

James Banks on Multicultural Education

From an interview by Anne Turnbaugh Lockwood in *Focus in Change*, published by the National Center for Effective Schools Research & Development (Banks, quoted in Lockwood 1992):

> The primary goal of multicultural education is an education for freedom. . . . Multicultural education should help students to develop the knowledge, attitudes, and skills to participate in a democratic and free society. . . . Multicultural education promotes the freedom, abilities and skills to cross ethnic and cultural boundaries to participation in other cultures and groups (p. 23).

> Multicultural education is for *all* children, not just for African Americans or Hispanics or Native Americans, but for all students (p. 23).

> In the multicultural classroom, students hear multiple voices and multiple perspectives. They hear the voice of different ethnic and cultural groups (p. 23).

> The aims of multicultural education should always be the same, regardless of the setting. However, the strategy points and methods may have to be contextualized (p. 26).

> Multicultural education is primarily a way of thinking. It's a way of asking questions, a way of conceptualizing. I would start with self-development, with new knowledge, with helping teachers ask questions about the materials they have (p. 27).

A multicultural curriculum can be taught with almost any materials if the teachers have the knowledge, skills, and attitudes needed to . . . transform their thinking and consequently the school curriculum (p. 27).

> Multicultural education is an inclusive and cementing movement. . . . It attempts to bring various groups that have been on the margins of society to the center of society (p. 27).

From an interview in *Teaching Tolerance*, a magazine distributed without charge by the Southern Law Poverty Center, Montgomery, Alabama (Banks 1992):

> Multicultural education is not about dividing a united nation, but about uniting a deeply divided nation (p. 21).

> Multiculturalism ultimately is a way of thinking. It's thinking about concepts from different people's vantage points. It's recognizing other perspectives. . . . It's caring, and taking action to make our society more just and humane (p. 22).

> Multicultural education is a reform movement designed to bring about educational equity for all students, including those from different races, ethnic groups, social classes, exceptionality, and sexual orientations (p. 21).

References

Banks, J.A. (1988). *Multiethnic Education: Theory and Practice.* 2nd ed. Boston: Allyn and Bacon.

Banks, J.A. (1991). *Teaching Strategies for Ethnic Studies.* 5th ed. Boston: Allyn and Bacon.

Banks, J.A. (December 1991/January 1992). "Multicultural Education: For Freedom's Sake." *Educational Leadership* 49, 4: 32–36.

Banks, J.A. (Fall 1992). "It's Up to Us." *Teaching Tolerance*, pp. 20–23.

Banks, J.A., and C.A. McGee Banks. (1991) *Multicultural Education: Issues and Perspectives.* Boston: Allyn and Bacon.

Lockwood, A.T. (Summer 1992). "Education for Freedom." *Focus in Change* 7: 23–29. (National Center for Effective Schools Research & Development).

Mack, C., Jr. (July-August 1992). "Mistaken Identity and Issues in Multicultural Education." *Updating School Board Policies* 23, 6: 1–4.

Nieto, S. (1992). *Affirming Diversity: The Sociopolitical Context of Multicultural Education.* White Plains, N.Y.: Longman.

2 Engaging Students in Evolving the Multicultural Classroom

Multicultural education is . . . *about* all people; it is also *for* all people, regardless of their ethnicity, language, religion, gender, race, or class.

> Sonia Nieto, *Affirming Diversity*
> (1992, p. 213)

Multicultural education . . . is a process that goes beyond the changing demographics in a particular country.

> Sonia Nieto, *Affirming Diversity*
> (1992, p. 220)

Teacher to Teacher

Now that you have some grounding in the theories behind multicultural education, how can you begin to evolve your multicultural classroom? Do you introduce students to the theories or do you go to the crux of the matter and involve them in examining their own multicultural identities? The theories support the fact that *everyone* is part of our ethnically diverse population and hence the constituency for which a multicultural education process is appropriate. But how can you start students on what will hopefully be a lifelong multicultural learning process?

As part of my own evolution as a multicultural educator, I have developed three exercises to get students (or teachers) into a multicultural mode—"Under the Multicultural Umbrella," "What Is Multiculturalism?" and "Naming Our Cultural Selves." They can be used separately or together or can serve as a basis for developing your own "Getting Started" strategy.

Strategy 1. Under the Multicultural Umbrella

"Drawing" Students into Multicultural Education

As I introduce middle school students to the concepts of cultural diversity and the goals of multicultural education, I use a visual "drawing" tool as a concrete way to help them understand the evolving sets of groups and concerns included under the "umbrella" of diversity. This strategy can also serve as an ongoing or pre/post assessment of students' understanding and critical-thinking skills.

Because the major thrust of multicultural education is sensitizing students to the unique needs and qualities of cultural groups, I begin by handing out large sheets of blank drawing paper and markers. I divide the students into teams of two to three students each. Then I ask my students to draw a huge beach or oversized umbrella. Once they have drawn the umbrellas, I tell them to label it "The Multicultural Umbrella." Next I challenge them to work in teams to generate lists of the groups who go under the umbrella. To help the students with their lists, I suggest the following categories (spokes of the multicultural umbrella): ethnic, racial, religious, cultural, and special needs/concerns. (See Section III, Worksheet 1, for a suggested process for "Under the Multicultural Umbrella.")

The students are given 5–10 minutes to generate their team lists. Then teams are asked to share the groups they have defined (or "art"iculated) with the whole class. Each group reads off their Umbrella's coverage. As each group presents, I encourage the other teams to react, reflect, and respond to the groups listed by other teams. The teams note those groups that appear under more than one team's Multicultural Umbrella. (See Figure 2.1 for a sample "Multicultural Umbrella" with various groups listed.)

Results of Pilot Studies Using the Umbrella

The "Multicultural Umbrella" strategy has been field tested by more than 300 middle school students across the United States (Oklahoma City, Oklahoma; Winston Salem, North Carolina; Wilmington, Delaware; Seattle, Washington; Portland, Oregon; Philadelphia, Pennsylvania; St. Louis, Missouri; and Santa Barbara, California, as well as Flushing, Washington Heights, Bensonhurst, Brooklyn, and the "Chinatown" area in New York City. The students' umbrellas sheltered different groups, depending on the location of their schools and other factors.

The ethnic, racial, religious, cultural, and special needs/special concerns groups most frequently listed by middle school students include black Americans (also referred to by the students as Afro-Americans), Hispanics/Latinos, Jews, Roman Catholics, Protestants, women, children, abandoned children, teens, police, physically challenged/handicapped, AIDS sufferers, Koreans, Chinese Americans, and Bosnians. Those groups taking refuge under the umbrella vary with the time period the umbrella is drawn and the groups who figure prominently in the news. For instance, women, Irish, gays, and lesbians appear under almost every Multicultural Umbrella list in March, but are often "left out" of lists made in January.

FIGURE 2.1
The Multicultural Umbrella

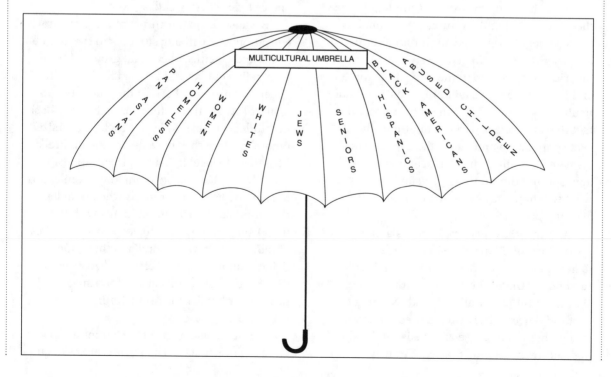

The range of cultural diversity and number of different ethnic, racial, religious, cultural, and special needs/special concerns groups initially placed under the Multicultural Umbrella also vary according to the neighborhood and school ethnic distribution of groups. When the strategy was introduced to students in New York City's Washington Heights schools, which are over 85 percent Dominican Republican, the students automatically included Dominican Republicans under their Umbrellas. These students quickly informed me that a "Hispanic" or "Latino" label was much too general. They felt that diverse groups had to be separated and specifically listed. They mentioned Puerto Ricans, Cubans, and Colombians. As a consequence of the ethnic breakdown of their own community school and immediate neighborhood, these students did not cite Koreans, Chinese, Muslims, Indians, or Jews. They included Irish because there is a small but significant Irish population in Washington Heights.

Students in multiethnic Flushing, Queens, put Chinese and Koreans under the Multicultural Umbrella, but never included Dominican Republicans per se, although some of their umbrellas had Hispanic or Latino groups listed. Again, this corresponded to the ethnic breakdown of their school population. In Bayside, Queens, Japanese were listed because some of these public schools had students who were either Japanese Americans or children of Japanese businessmen who were visiting the United States. In general, because of the broad range of diversity represented in Flushing—which includes sixty-four distinct language/ethnic groups—the students' initial Multicultural Umbrellas covered many different groups.

In contrast to the Flushing students, those in some of the more homogeneous Chinatown schools, where most students were from Chinese backgrounds with only a few black or Latino students, listed very few groups under their umbrellas. When the strategy was field tested in another site—a Wilmington, Delaware, parochial school with 100 percent white, middle-class students from Polish and Italian backgrounds—their Multicultural Umbrellas sheltered few groups. Students in Oklahoma City included specific Native American tribes under their umbrellas because of the numbers of Native Americans in their communities. On the other hand, students in a St. Louis, Missouri, public school had difficulty in going beyond blacks, whites, and Hispanics. When a few students finally volunteered Jews, Koreans, and Chinese as groups, another student said: "Oh, those are New York City groups—they're not important in St. Louis."

Using the Umbrella to Sensitize Students

The students' initial drawing and articulating of their Multicultural Umbrellas also highlighted for me, as a teacher and as a citizen, some of their (and the general adult public's) misconceptions about the basic tenets of multicultural education. I told my 5th–8th graders that the evolving definitions of which groups were included under the Multicultural Umbrella were the work of several key scholars in the field. One theorist whose name and ideas (in selected quote form) I shared with them was James Banks (see Chapter 1). I told them that this gentleman was "the guru" of multicultural education. I gave the students a sheet with quotes I had extracted from the works of Banks and other researchers (see Figures 1.1 and 1.2).

Then, referring to the umbrellas the students had drawn (which were posted with masking tape on the blackboard), I threw out some "devil's advocate" questions designed to focus the class as a whole on multicultural issues implicit in the umbrella.

Pointing to myself and identifying myself as a Caucasian Jewish woman, I asked the students if whites were a group to be included under the umbrella. Depending on the site, ethnic composition, and past multicultural discussion experiences of the class, some of the students were a bit thrown by this question. Several shook their heads no. Occasionally, students would explain that the Multicultural Umbrella was designed to protect the needs of persons of color. The students were asked to review Banks' selected quotes. They then realized that the Multicultural Umbrella is designed to shelter the needs of *all* persons.

Next, I asked the students to look at the posted lists and see which special needs/special concerns groups were left out. Because the combined team lists in the New York City Public schools once were fairly extensive, the students were often hard put to come up with a group they hadn't already included under the Multicultural Umbrella. Ironically, the frequent omission of senior citizens was the single constant factor that surfaced in the broad geographic spectrum of school sites surveyed. However, once the omission of this group was pointed out to students, they were able to see why this constituency needed the protection of the Multicultural Umbrella.

Another special needs group that was infrequently mentioned by students (with the exception of students in New York City—and even these had to be somewhat prompted) were the homeless. I would try to elicit inclusion of the homeless, AIDS sufferers, people with terminal illnesses, and battered (abused) children by telling the students that the Multicultural Umbrella was designed to shelter those groups whose members suffer social, legal, or economic discrimination. Using this criterion as a prompt, most groups of students were able to include many other special needs categories under the umbrella.

To sensitize the students to the fact that the ethnic, racial, religious, and special needs groupings under the umbrella are not mutually exclusive, I asked the students whether they could think of a situation where an individual could be a member of more than one group under the umbrella at the same time. The students very quickly came up with the following: a homeless female senior citizen, a teenage black AIDS sufferer, an abused baby, a terminally ill teenager, and a battered Italian senior citizen.

Using the Umbrella in Integrated Curriculums

The Multicultural Umbrella graphics served as growing focal points for my middle school students' ongoing multiculturally themed, integrated language arts studies. As part of our "Newspapers in Education" studies, the students included the increasingly diverse ethnic, racial, religious, and special needs groups whose concerns were the focus of media coverage. The students wrote reflective essays about the quality, intensity, objectivity, and impact of the diversity coverage. They also wrote letters to the editor and developed surveys to explore how their peers and communities reacted to coverage of multicultural groups.

In addition to listing the groups under the original Multicultural Umbrella, students also mapped the ethnic and language groups covered on an outline world map and discussed which regions received the greatest media attention at what time. They explored how geographic location influenced the status and needs of various cultural groups.

As part of the process of identifying and including various groups under the Multicultural Umbrella, the students realized that many had different names. *Black Americans* were also known as *African Americans; whites* were also called *Caucasians*. The term *Hispanic* was preferred by some individuals whom others called *Latino*. The individuals identified as *handicapped* were also listed as *physically challenged*. My students compiled a multicultural dictionary that included specific (aka) designations for various cultural groups, as well as detailed listings of specific Latino, Pan Asian, and Native American (indigenous peoples) groups.

In one of the New York City middle schools where the "Multicultural Umbrella" was piloted, the black American students did an oral history project in which they and their parents examined which ethnic "name" was a "preferred" one and how the designation for black Americans had evolved over the past sixty years. Inspired by our success with this "spoke" on our original "Multicultural Umbrella," students pursued other oral histories on the theme of "A rose by any other name"—exploring various terms for Jews (Semites, Zionists), Hispanics, and Pan Asians. As part of these investigations, the students in each of the multicultural groups began to think about how they wanted to refer to themselves culturally.

As a follow-up to the Umbrella activity, I modified a strategy I encountered at a citywide Multicultural Institute, where teachers in small groups were asked to write a definition of multicultural education. I extended this idea and used it with the middle school students. After we had been involved in the Umbrella study, I asked the students to use their original team-developed Multicultural Umbrellas, maps, and writings to evolve a "working definition" of multicultural education. Their team definitions were as insightful, rich, and evocative as the ones the adult teachers had developed at the Multicultural Institute. Among them:

> Multicultural education means learning about the needs and skills of many groups, whose numbers and names sometimes change. But the fact that everyone under the Multicultural Umbrella deserves respect does not change.

> The Multicultural Umbrella just keeps on expanding as more groups need the protection of rights, responsibility, and self-pride.

> Under the Multicultural Umbrella, all subjects include parents, community, students, and teachers sharing their backgrounds. Everyone huddles together. The Multicultural Umbrella helps them stay safe and sound.

Just like its oversized prototype in real life, the "Multicultural Umbrella" strategy served to draw my students and me into a broad spectrum of culturally centered civic studies. We will continue to meet under its auspices to probe cultural concerns.

> In the multicultural classroom, students hear multiple voices and multiple perspectives. They hear the voice of different ethnic and cultural groups.
> Banks (quoted in Lockwood 1992, p. 23)

Strategy 2. What Is Multiculturalism?

A Pre-Course Survey Tool for Teachers

As I planned an inservice course for K–8 teachers in "Creating Materials for a Diverse Classroom"—a title suggested by someone who felt "Multicultural Strategies" was too controversial—I designed a survey that confronted the so-called controversy head on, but allowed the teachers to share their their feelings and reflections anonymously. Strategy 2, "What Is Multiculturalism?" is a kind of litmus test or assessment—a reflection piece that poses questions for those beginning an in-depth study of multicultural education. (See Section III, Worksheet 2, for a copy of the survey.)

The teachers were given two copies of the survey. They were told that they would hand one in without a signature at the close of the first session, but keep the second one for themselves to review and annotate at the end of the course. I gave the teachers 20 minutes to fill out the surveys and reflect on them.

Some teachers just sat quietly, while others wrote intently. Several asked for more time and were given it.

After I collected the unsigned surveys, I encouraged the group to discuss the issues raised by the survey, focusing attention on the issue of whether multicultural education should be taught only by ethnically diverse educators.

Many felt that this question was particularly relevant in an ethnically diverse district, whose teaching staff was overwhelmingly over forty and white. Discussion among the participants was frank, but at least one-third of the group had no comments. I sat quietly, but listened to the exchange.

The group moved on to cover the issue of whether the multicultural education thrust was just the current buzzword or a new term for an aspect of curriculum that teachers were already infusing. Again, I was not surprised that a group of veteran teachers would opt to consider the significance and applicability of the multicultural movement. What was interesting was that, again, only a small percentage of individuals offered their views.

In contrast to the limited participation in our open discussion, my review of the survey showed that the webbing and drawing associations, as well as the questions about who should teach multicultural courses and the multicultural aspects of curriculum, evoked the most varied and detailed responses. About a third of the participants left the "alternative lifestyles" and "intergroup tensions" questions blank.

By the end of the course, the participants filled in all the questions and associations on the survey. They made detailed annotations on their original reflections and assessed the changes in their perceptions of multicultural education.

Use of the Survey with Middle Schoolers

I adapted the format of the pre/post assessment for a class of 7th graders who were working on a student-written news broadcast that featured a commentary on the "Controversial Aspects of Multicultural Education." Among the issues that had been raised in New York City in the fall of 1992 were:

• Inclusion of discussion of alternative lifestyles and family units in the primary grades;
• The appropriateness of a teacher-prepared bibliography that included early childhood books with positive stories about gay lifestyles; and

• The implementation of a multicultural curriculum in schools with intergroup tensions.

Unlike the teachers who had completed this survey previously, the 7th graders were mostly ethnically diverse, with at least 10 percent coming from new-immigrant, non-native-English-speaking homes. They wrote and drew intently. Several added sheets of blank paper to the one-page survey, which we sent for copying so one unsigned copy could be collected and one copy kept by the students.

The students also contrasted with the adult teachers in their overwhelming embrace of multicultural education. One emotionally said:

> Just do it! . . . Really talk about race and culture in class! Stop preparing lessons, let's get to it!

Other students opened up about being victims of mockery or feeling like nonpersons in certain groups. Another student shared how her native Indian dress made her teachers, some fellow students, and a school secretary uncomfortable. Their response had made her begin to question whether she "belonged" in the school and start "pressuring" her parents to let her drop her native dress, which in turn upset them. Finally, one student asked me how the teachers' Multicultural Inservice course was going. "They're the ones who really need this. They don't understand students from different backgrounds."

Yet when I picked up on this theme by asking the students their view on whether multicultural units or themes were best taught by teachers "of color" or "ethnically diverse" backgrounds, the class was divided. Some of their responses were:

> That's a kind of separate but equal teacher segregation. It insults diverse students and teachers.

No, I like being taught by a teacher from my own background. It gives me a role model.

I would like to have a Pakistani teacher. It would make me proud. That teacher could help me learn.

But I wouldn't want a teacher to be hired only or mostly on the basis of ethnicity. I once got picked for a special program on that basis. To tell the truth, I was sort of ashamed, even though I wanted to be in the group. That's the downside of this multicultural movement.

We didn't settle the questions in either of the parallel teacher and student multicultural education courses, but both groups' perceptions of the concerns involved in multicultural education were enriched. The "What Is Multiculturalism?" survey or assessment tool, with its mix of visual and verbal associations and open-ended questions, helped students, teachers, and me assess their views and evolving stands on the issues inherent in multicultural studies. Given the visceral academic, political, and educational ramifications of this movement, the tool can serve other students and adult analysts in their examination and development of courses for addressing diversity.

Strategy 3.
Naming Our Cultural Selves

Engaging middle school and secondary school students in the process of multicultural, interdisciplinary education is a formidable challenge. In a conventional approach, teachers can present students with basic principles of multicultural theories from the works of James Banks (1988, 1991, 1992; see also Banks and Banks 1991) and Sonia Nieto (1992) or ask them to map out their ethnic and cultural backgrounds. This approach will indeed provide the student with background research and content in diversity; however, it does not help students

put the process into context. More important, these essentially linguistic and spatial activities do not provide what Howard Gardner (1991) calls "entry" points to multicultural studies for interpersonal, intrapersonal, auditory (musical), logical-mathematical, and kinesthetic learning—some of the multiple intelligences that Gardner has identified. Adding technology to the process does allow for kinesthetic, spatial, and other learning. To provide such multiple entry points, as well as to facilitate immediate, whole-language-supported connections with multicultural thinking, I have piloted and refined a strategy to involve students in the context of their cultures. This strategy consists of inviting students to give themselves cultural names and provide feedback to the class and the teacher (Routman 1991). (For a copy of the student worksheet, "Naming Our Cultural Selves," see Section III, Worksheet 3.)

An Invitation to Naming

I began by providing my students with an open "invitation" to "name" their cultural selves. By way of introduction, I offered an example of the "naming" process with excerpts from T.S. Eliot's poem "The Naming of Cats" (*Old Possum's Book of Practical Cats*. New York: Harvest, 1939):

The naming of cats is a difficult matter,
It isn't just one of your holiday games . . .
You may think at first I'm mad as a hatter
When I tell you, a cat must have three
  different names
First of all, there's the name the family
  may use daily . . .

A cat needs a name that's particular,
A name that's peculiar, and more
  dignified . . .
Names that never belong to more than
  one cat.

But above and beyond there's still one
  name left over . . .
The name that no human research can

discover—
But The Cat Himself Knows, and will
   never confess.
His ineffable effable
Effanineffable
Deep and inscrutable singular name. . . .

The students began their own private "Naming" files on the computer, and then they identified the three "names" of the cats: "family name," "personal peculiar name," and the name known only to the cat—the "ineffable effable . . . singular name." They first defined from context the words "ineffable," "effable"/ "effanineffable," "inscrutable," and "singular." These "personally arrived at" definitions were shared and printed out. Finally, the students looked up and added the dictionary definitions to their own contextually derived ones.

Teacher's Response

Then I asked the students to focus on the three "levels" of names T.S. Eliot listed for cats. I suggested that they "think" in their heads whether this three-tiered naming process holds in our personal lives as well. As they reflected, I shared my personal responses with the students (I read the following paragraphs aloud, as well as provided a printout):

"Name that the family uses daily . . . Sensible everyday names . . ."

In my personal birth family, I am called by my English birth certificate name Rose Cherie. . . . I'm named for my maternal grandmother, Rose, who passed away before I was born. The French "Cherie" for *dear* was my father's idea. I am her Hebrew namesake, as well, and thus take the place vacated by her passing among the living Jewish community members. Her Hebrew name was Haya Rais, which translates to *Living Animal* (Haya) *Rose* (Raisel). My family calls me this, as well. I also have a Yiddish nickname, Rosh, which is a contracted version of my birth name Rose Cherie and also a Hebrew word for "head," as in *smart*.

"A name that's particular, a name that's peculiar, and more dignified . . ."

My students, editors, professional colleagues, neighborhood business owners, the postman, and other outsiders call me "Mrs. Reissman," "Ms. Reissman," or "Teacher" or "Teach." I'm proud to answer to these names, which "name" my relationship to my family, my profession, and my community.

"One name left over . . . ineffable, effable/effanineffable/deep and inscrutable singular name . . ."

That's really tough. . . . I guess you have to think about what you call or think of yourself, as when you reflect or focus on yourself. For me, there's not one single name but a few. . . . I think of myself as Rosh or Haya (*living animal*). I also know I am "Yid"—a Jew. These names are my most cultural birth names and the name often ascribed, sometimes in hatred, to my religious group. I find the "Jewish" aspect of me to be most deeply personal.

Students' Responses

After I finished my own process of naming, I asked the students what they had learned about me as a person from listening to me think through my "naming" steps. I told them they could read through the printout of my response, and that they could enter their reactions in their computer file, print them out, and share them with me, rather than tell them to the class. At least one-third of the students took that option! Among the responses of the various classes with whom I have piloted this technique are:

You most identify as a Jew. There're Hebrew ideas in you, even more than your regular American names.

You like all your different names. I hate my "real" Chinese name and I feel uncomfortable when it's used at home. I like that my friends, Chinese and American, call me Phil.

Although I am a Latino, I certainly wouldn't say that is part of any name for myself, but I guess I would have to put that in my family name and "name that's particular" name. As Octavian Rodriguez, I can't very well hope to be treated as anything other than a Latino. Being a Latino today sucks [exact student expression]!

I dropped my Vietnamese birth name Somtook when I was in second grade . . . . No one could even pronounce it. Even if the teacher finally learned it, most of the other kids laughed at me. "Sam," my English name, is easy to say. My family still calls me Somtook at home. But you know, deep down I call "me" Somtook too! I guess it is my "ineffable effable" . . . name. Maybe even if the rest of the world accepts your American name, your birth name and your birth identity is still the name you call yourself.

My parents are very proud Protestants. My middle name is Jesus. We are also a proud Black American family whose ancestors were African kings. When I was born my dad insisted on calling me Darius. At home they call me Darius every day, but use the full Darius Jesus at the Church, Kwanza, and special events. I guess I buy into some of my family's cultural values because when I think about the "me" myself, I think about "Emperor Darius." So "Emperor Darius" is my most personal name.

The use of the "private" computer files, the quiet of the lab, and my own initial responses to the invitation facilitated my students' very personal reflective responses.

One of the most touching and upsetting responses to my spoken self-revelation was a printout left on my desk after a session where many students had gone through the "Naming Our Cultural Selves" process orally, and a rich

discussion of shared reflections had just concluded. The printout said:

This class made me feel very out of things. I am living with foster parents. I don't remember my real mom or dad. My name was given to me by my first foster parents who I haven't seen. But my child is going to know who he or she is and what the name he gets means. Maybe my child will have an easier time naming himself than I have. The "naming" is great . . . and I will "name" myself. . . . The naming of self is the most important . . . Right??

Both the students' comments and this written note confirmed for me the value in providing multiethnic students with auditory (musical), intrapersonal, and interpersonal entry points to multicultural studies. Through sharing of my own and the students' personal responses, we were able to place complex issues into context—for both group and individual identification. Whole-language emphasis on oral language and retelling of family traditions was an integral part of this first stage of conversations about diversity. As the students and I shared our families', communities', and individual responses to "naming" ourselves, we role-played multiple perspectives. Sometimes the students had decided which perspective they accepted. Other students were still in the process of choosing the "inscrutable ineffable name" they would call themselves. Some students had changed their *self* names.

Extensions of the Cultural Naming Process

Following our "talking" and "telling" (oral language, intrapersonal, interpersonal), I invited the students to write out the naming process (see "Naming Our Cultural Selves" in Section III, Worksheet 3) or to draw it out using drawing software to create storyboards, shields, or family trees. The students were allowed to choose any of these options or more than one, if they were so inclined and had time. The options they selected allowed them to articulate our original oral language findings and demonstrate their responses in a way (Routman 1991) that was most suited to their individual, multiple-intelligence learning "entry points" (Gardner 1991). Thus the spatial learners characteristically designed storyboards, shields, and family trees to represent their names; and one student wrote a "shape" poem.

One student used *MacDraw*[R] to combine logical-mathematical and spatial intelligences into a unique graphic naming "structure," which also needed verbal explanation as it was shared (interpreted) for the class. Several students put together mixed-media "naming" slide shows, including slides, baby pictures, cultural tokens, and music effects, to share their "naming processes." These performance pieces were greatly appreciated by an engaged peer audience.

In response to the note I had received from the student who didn't know the origins of her name and to students who didn't want to interpersonally share their cultural and family reflections, I offered other options for expression. Students could interview family or community members, school staff, and peers from other classes. They and their interview subjects could then decide how to present or articulate the subjects' "naming" reflections. This option worked out very well, because the interviewers were able to "produce" their "outsider" naming findings for their peers. They also gained valuable insights into how other individuals "named" themselves. One student, who worked in a community service after-school project at a neighborhood senior center, gave out the worksheet we had used to the seniors. The class and the seniors were pleased by the results. Two seniors visited the class to share their photos, baptismal certificates, I.D. cards, and memories.

By using technology to facilitate talking, drawing, reflecting, interviewing, reacting, producing media presentations, collecting "name" artifacts, building, and designing, students can be immersed in a rich, interdisciplinary, "naming" inquiry. The use of technology guarantees student privacy and offers those with particular spatial, kinesthetic, and auditory (musical) intelligences a private tool for participating in this introspective activity. "Naming Our Cultural Selves" is a technology-supported learning activity that enables students to use multiple intelligences in active, whole-language experiences. This strategy can serve as a standing introduction to living and participating in a diverse society.

Assessment in the Multicultural Classroom

Although the focus of this book is evolving multidisciplinary curriculums that infuse multicultural understandings into the process of school and lifelong learning, assessment procedures are inherent in the various strategies presented. Indeed, if the teacher's goal is to monitor the effectiveness of these activities, then performance, publication, portfolio, project, and community outreach assessment tools can easily be set up.

In this chapter, I have included detailed discussions of two important pre/post assessments—"Under the Multicultural Umbrella" and "What Is Multiculturalism?"—that can be used in the process of engaging students (and teachers) in multicultural education. Section II, "Curriculum Strategies," includes references to many different kinds of assessments that teachers and students can use.

Most of the multicultural curriculum strategies discussed here involve student products, projects, exhibits, peer reviews, performances, and community activities. I have included an assessment chart (Figure 2.2) that shows a sampling of strategies and the assessments that can be used with each, including an indication of ongoing evaluations.

FIGURE 2.2

Assessment Chart for Sample Multicultural Strategies

1. Under the Multicultural Umbrella*   **
   (Chapter 2, Engaging Students)

2. What Is Multiculturalism?*   **   ***
   (Chapter 2, Engaging Students)

3. Cresting for Character and Community*   ***
   (Chapter 3, Multicultural Language Arts)

4. Storyboarding Reader Response*   **   ***
   (Chapter 3, Multicultural Language Arts)

5. Leaving Out to Pull In*   ***
   (Chapter 3, Multicultural Language Arts)

6. Cultural Collages*   **   ***
   (Chapter 4, Multicultural Social Studies)

7. Bills of Responsibilities*   **   ***
   (Chapter 4, Multicultural Social Studies)

8. First Ladies in Profile (F.L.I.P.)*   **   ***
   (Chapter 4, Multicultural Social Studies)

9. Geocurrents*   **   ***
   (Chapter 4, Multicultural Social Studies)

10. Cultural Greeting Cards*   **   ***
    (Chapter 5, Multidisciplinary Multicultural Arts)

1. Spatial/linguistic pre/post cognitive assessment; peer review; team processing and evaluation

2. Pre/post cognitive and attitudinal assessment for teachers, parents, community members, and students

3. Peer reviews (class, on-line); critiquing; community outreach and feedback (exhibits, festivals); performance; portfolios; oral communication

4. Peer reviews (class, on-line); critiquing; community outreach (exhibits, festivals, peer teaching); performance; portfolios of artwork and creative writing

5. Student comparison to teacher/printed text; student writings; student applications of strategy to independent work; portfolios

6. Pre/post cognitive assessment; peer review; portfolios; exhibits; community feedback

7. Publications (computer/printing); performance/community evaluation; portfolios; logs of appropriate cases to consider; student writing; peer review; feedback from special interest groups; forums; community feedback

8. Desktop-published trading cards; peer/community feedback; process portfolios; portfolios of student artwork and creative writing; exhibits; improvisations; peer review; student-developed assessments

9. Portfolios of appropriate pieces; peer review; publications; exhibits; performances; competitions; student-developed assessments

10. Peer assessment of cards; community feedback; exhibits; peer on-line sharing (plus oral communication); desktop publication of cards; portfolios of artwork and creative writing; critiques

*   Peer assessed
**   Ongoing throughout the year
*** Placed in a dated portfolio or computer file/portfolio

References

Banks, J.A. (1988). *Multiethnic Education: Theory and Practice.* 2nd ed. Newton, Mass.: Allyn and Bacon.

Banks, J.A. (1991). *Teaching Strategies for Ethnic Studies.* 5th ed. Boston: Allyn and Bacon.

Banks, J.A., and C.A. McGee Banks, eds. (1991). *Multicultural Education: Issues and Perspectives.* Needham Heights, Mass.: Allyn and Bacon.

Gardner, H. (1991). *The Unschooled Mind.* New York: Basic Books.

Gardner, H. (1993). *Multiple Intelligences.* New York: Basic Books.

Lockwood, A.T. (Summer 1992). "Education for Freedom." *Focus in Change* 7: 23–29. (National Center for Effective Schools Research & Development).

Nieto, S. (1992). *Affirming Diversity—The Sociopolitical Context of Multicultural Education.* New York: Longman.

Routman, R. (1991). *Invitations: Changing as Teachers and Learners, K–12.* Portsmouth, N.H.: Heinemann.

SECTION II

CURRICULUM STRATEGIES

3 Multicultural Language Arts

Teacher to Teacher

Teachers may have questions about how multicultural education fits in with strategies used in their language arts programs, such as whole language, reader response, and multiple intelligences:

Okay, this multicultural education process is really relevant to me and my students, but I have a problem in infusing it. You see, I'm in a school that's dedicated to the whole language movement.

My chairperson is very strong on reader response theories. How can I work the multicultural education process into those theories?

Our school is working with Howard Gardner's Multiple Intelligences theory. How can I mesh multicultural education with that research?

With all the movements on the research forefront and the commitment of various schools and English/Language Arts departments to one or another, including the multicultural process may appear to be burdensome or even impossible. But on reflection, the multicultural process is compatible with the research and theory initiatives that are in place in many middle and secondary schools.

Benefits of Infusing Multicultural Perspectives into Language Arts

Most teachers have long understood the benefits to their students of providing for multicultural perspectives in language arts. Indeed, many current textbooks and curriculums make special efforts to include works from cultures other than the dominant U.S., Western culture. But there are other reasons to include such perspectives—including the reinforcement of strategies currently used by excellent teachers: whole language strategies, reader response theory, and the multiple intelligences theory of Howard Gardner (1983, 1991, 1993).

A Complement to Whole Language

Among the key tenets or principles of the whole language movement (Goodman 1986, Routman 1991) are:

• Each student has something special to contribute.
• Communication takes place all the time between student and students, teacher and students.
• Learning is based on real-world news and information.
• Engagement in purposeful activities is based on real-world material.
• Personal interest material is used as a resource for language.
• Peer collaboration/learning is a social event.

Each of these tenets is completely consistent with and supportive of the multicultural education process—and vice versa.

The quintessence of multicultural education is the inclusion and celebration of every students' capacities, cultural background, and uniqueness. Hence its goals are quite congruent with the whole language tenet "Each student has something special to contribute." The multicultural education process occurs through a series of student/student and teacher/student conversations about cultures. These conversations are exactly the type of communications advocated by the whole language movement.

If "learning is [to be] based on real-world news and information," what better or more necessary information than an exploration and examination of factual, authentic information about cultures? What could be more purposeful, real-world learning than the alleviation of culturally caused conflicts through real-world news and information? Multiculturalism and whole language can effectively work together to attain goals that are mutually reinforcing.

If students engage in Banks' (1991) social action approach to multicultural education, wherein they write letters, draft bills, assist senior citizens, and work on community issues, are they not "engaged in purposeful writing and purposeful activities based on the real world"? Of course. So in integrating ethnic content across the curriculum, students are also attaining whole language goals.

Through study of students' own cultural backgrounds, stories, histories, customs, and mythologies, the multicultural education process uses "personal interest material as a resource for language." Again, both movements enrich, strengthen, and realize one another's goals.

Finally, through its focus on intercultural, peer-group conversations, multicultural education nurtures "peer collaboration and learning as a social event"—including a specific Banks

social-action approach for engaging the community.

So much for worries over how to infuse multicultural methodologies into a whole language approach. Not only is it possible, but infusion of a multicultural process and goals into a whole language environment will strengthen both initiatives, as well as enhance student goals for each. All the language arts strategies presented in this section could be used as part of a whole language initiative. For example, the "Atlas Cards" strategy encourages students to pursue personal interests while engaging in collaborative, cooperative projects related to real life.

Reinforcement of Reader Response

In much the same way, multicultural education processes and reader response theory are mutually supportive. Louise Rosenblatt's reader response theories (1976, 1978) are strongly rooted in the concept that every reader brings her own background and prior reactions/experiences to a text; likewise, through multicultural education, students explore their own perspectives on literature. Indeed, five strategies described in this chapter ("Oral History—Family Chats," "Reaching Out, Reaching In," "Leaving Out to Pull In," "Multicultural Peer Portraits," and "F.A.L.L. Into Literature") are rooted in reader response theory.

Focus on Multiple Intelligences

On the surface, Howard Gardner's theories (1983, 1991, 1993) of the seven multiple intelligences would appear to be different in orientation from the multicultural process needed to evolve the multicultural classroom. Gardner's focus on engaging individual intelligence capacities as "entry points" for learning, however, is consistent with the multicultural celebration of individual uniqueness, as well as group commonalities. The language arts activities in this chapter address specific multiple intelligence capacities. The "Oral History—Family Chats" and

"Reaching Out, Reaching In" strategies, particularly, specifically use intrapersonal and interpersonal intelligences, with strands of linguistic (interviews, conversations) and spatial (photos/memorabilia exhibits) intelligences.

Two strategies, "F.A.L.L. Into Literature" and "Leaving Out to Pull In," are essentially linguistic intelligence activities, with both intrapersonal and interpersonal threads. In contrast, four strategies, "Storyboarding Reader Response," "Cresting for Character and Community," "Atlas Cards," and "Showing Peer Portraits" are a mix of spatial and linguistic content entry points. (See Section III for worksheets for these strategies.) If viewed through the perspective of multiple intelligence theory, multicultural language arts can be used effectively as a tool for providing multiple-intelligence entry points to instruction.

Strategy 4. Oral History— Family Chats

An Argument for Introducing Oral History on a K–3 Level

As a lifelong lover of the oral history tradition, I have always integrated oral history components into my elementary and middle school social studies and language arts curriculums. In activities as diverse as voter registration, book censorship, memories of schools from twenty/thirty years ago, comparative constitutional rights study, and teaching styles, the infusion of oral history has meaningfully engaged parents and community members in classroom studies, as well as validated our projects for my students. Yet, as many of my elementary school colleagues point out, the oral history approach seems to be inapplicable on the early childhood (K–3) level, because children at these young ages lack proficiency in necessary interviewing, writing, and communication skills. In addition, contemplation of history, even reflections on events of the immediate past (a year

or two ago), is beyond the cognitive maturity level of this age group.

Despite these limitations, I have found viable strategies for integrating oral history techniques and projects into younger children's K–3 educational experiences. Consider some questions that teachers might ask:

1. *But younger students can't "record" oral histories, since they haven't yet mastered note-taking or interviewing. What connection can or do they make with history?*

Although the majority of K–3 students can't "take written notes" during an interview, they can "draw" images and events discussed. Most K–3 students use tape recorders as part of their own play and story "writing." Therefore, they can use drawing and taping to record their oral histories. After all, adult reporters, sketch artists, and some authors use these same devices.

2. *How can you expect young children to generate questions and then listen to the subject? Can they develop additional questions based on the subject's response? Wouldn't you agree that that level of critical thinking is beyond the capacity of young children?*

If the oral history topic is one that relates to a young child's experiences and interests, K–3 students are good at asking questions.

3. *But what significant oral history topics could there be on young children's experience and interest levels?*

Many topics offer young children an opportunity to share or derive their learning from interaction with parents and community members. For example, children's first day of school and their feelings on this day remain vivid in the minds of young children.

"First Day at School" Oral History Project

To introduce oral history to K–3 students, you might ask the students to draw or tell about their feelings on their first day at school. For the purposes of this oral history inquiry, "first day at school" can refer to any school-type experience the children have had: day care center, preschool, kindergarten, play group, or kids' gym/dance program. All the children should be given a chance to talk about their first day, or show any drawings they have made about it. Then you can tell the children that although you are now much older than they are, once long ago you were also a little child going to school. You should then ask the students if they have any questions about what you felt about your first day at school. As the children raise various questions, you should repeat each one aloud before it is answered and then write down the questions on the blackboard or a large experiential chart. Young children have generated the following questions for teacher-initiated "First Day of School Oral Histories" (see also Worksheet 4 in Section III).

- How old were you when you started school?
- What did your classroom look like?
- Were you afraid to go to school? Why?
- What happened when you got into school?
- Was the teacher nice?
- Did you get hurt by the other kids? Did you get hit by other kids?
- Did you cry? Why?
- Were you afraid nobody would come for you?
- What did you do in school?
- Did you get to go to the bathroom?
- Did you ever have an accident in class?
- Did the kids make fun of you?
- Did you like school when you first got there?
- Did you like it later?

A review of these questions shows that young children do not use follow-up or linked questioning techniques, such as asking about the school schedule after asking "What did you do in school?" To encourage the children to use probing questions, draw the children into the linking question by saying: "Is there anything else you want to hear about?" Pause for them to generate another follow-through question. Be sure to put it on the blackboard or experiential chart next to the initial student-generated question.

Although this procedure may slow down the class's actual recording of the oral history, it models oral history questionnaire development and interviewing strategies for young children. This process experience is necessary if they are to eventually develop listening and interviewing skills beyond a class-generated interview questionnaire.

While sharing your own "First Day at School" oral history with the children, you should ask the children to draw or record your oral history. The drawings should be posted, and the children's recordings should be placed in a special center of the room. When the children have completed the drawings and tapes and have arranged them in the display area, you should congratulate the children on becoming oral historians.

Explain to the children that in the process of their having questioned, sketched, listened to, and recorded the teacher's memories, they have become part of a large group of children and adults who go around talking to people about topics that interest them. Ask the students if they can think of other adults or children whose stories about the first day of school they would like to hear. Among the individuals whose stories one group wanted to hear were: My grandmother's/grandfather's (several students named a grandparent), the principal's, the mayor's, an older sibling's, the school crossing guard's, my mother's, and my dad's.

Young children can interview some of these individuals at home and bring back a tape or drawings and assorted memorabilia from their subjects to be included in the First Day at School Oral History Center. Among the items on display in one Grade 2 First Day at School exhibit were photos of the subjects at school, a picture book from the first school experience, a report card from the first year of school, notes sent home from school, and a student-made storybook of that first day.

Some teachers might be concerned that the initial topics and therefore the young children's oral history projects would be very limited in scope and interdisciplinary content. After all, by necessity, they'll mostly be interviewing family and local community members. That dovetails nicely with the early-childhood "Community" curriculum, but it doesn't use oral history techniques to broaden young children's content knowledge and understandings beyond the standard curriculum.

The actual content knowledge and understandings, of course, will vary according to the ethnic composition of the particular school and neighborhood community. In the New York City public elementary schools, where young children are drawn from multiethnic, diverse backgrounds, the range of "First Day at School" experiences is quite global and infuses cross-cultural understandings into the standard curriculum. Among these are: lack of preschool or first day experience in Vietnam, late school starts in homes with withdrawal after 5th grade, parochial school 1st grade experience, at home/self-schooling, abandonment of a day-care center, six "First Day" experiences because a family moved around, and a one-room schoolhouse experience in Appalachia.

Other Oral History Topics

What topics or inquiries beyond the first day of school are accessible and of interest to young children? The topics are infinite. As children become more experienced in interviewing skills, they generate further topics as an outgrowth of initial inquiry. Among the primary oral history topics suggested by young children are:

- Toys of the past (by which they mean what their parents and grandparents played with)
- Birthday celebrations
- Ways of learning to read, do things, or make things in other countries
- Favorite stories
- Worst nightmares, other dreams
- Games you played when you were my age
- What was I like when I was a baby?
- What did you look like/act like when you were in grade ___?
- Hurricanes/snowstorms you experienced
- Accidents you had when you were my age
- Fights you had with other kids
- Favorite foods, foods you hated to eat
- Fears when you were my age
- Your dreams/hopes (children always want to know if they came true)

The range of interests that young children have in initiating oral histories offers classroom teachers a chance to use these activities to nurture and support student self-concept, self-esteem, skill development, and knowledge acquisition. The nature of the oral discussions, community participation, exhibits, and student products also lends credibility to ongoing assessments of children's progress.

Teachers can also use this interest in oral histories to launch children into lifelong, proactive cultural inquiries and social concerns. Such early initiatives can only serve to promote positive, informed, proactive citizenship and lifelong learning.

Strategy 5.
Reaching Out, Reaching In

Community-School Networking—
A Mutually Enriching Personal Experience

I don't like talking about my childhood or my Holocaust experiences. I've never joined one of those survivors' groups. Maybe other people need to light candles or weep, but not me. I look to the future.

This section is adapted from "Reaching Out . . . Reaching In: Story of the Holocaust," *English Journal*, September 1992. Copyright © 1992 by the National Council of Teachers of English. Adapted by permission.

Anyway, twelve-year-old children couldn't possibly understand what it was like to grow up in a camp. You expect too much of them. They're too young. They aren't Jews. It won't mean anything to them.

This was Adolf Lenz's (his real name) initial reaction to my request that he share his Holocaust experiences with my 6th graders. Adolf, who was a cab driver, and I had become friends after a cab ride. When we chatted, I learned we were neighbors—and I told him about my visiting many schools within one school day on a tight schedule. I recruited him to pick me up at various sites. Although Adolf actually lost potential fares on the days he assisted me, both of us enjoyed talking about city politics, education, and social issues. I would often share the children's ongoing projects with him. He was extremely interested in their radio shows and trips. He volunteered to pick up guests for our events and take them home, as well.

About a year into our friendship, I told Adolf that my students were reading Anne Frank's diary in preparation for visiting a special exhibit. I mentioned that I would try to get some Holocaust survivors who had been children during the 1940s to share their experiences with the class. It was then that Adolf told me he had survived a concentration camp, but adamantly rejected my invitation to talk to the class.

Adolf's response was so uncharacteristically harsh and negative that I pulled back. I felt that sharing these memories of his childhood was something Adolf could not do, perhaps even with his own family. Therefore, I was touched when the very next day, Adolf handed me an envelope of faded photographs. They were pictures of Adolf as a child. He said: "This is me when I left the camp at age five. This is my father. He carried me to freedom. This one is my mother. She died in the camp before my fifth birthday. I never cried for her."

As I looked over the pictures, I searched for the right words. Ever the teacher, I repressed my immediate feeling that seeing these photos of a Holocaust child who had survived to adulthood would enrich my students' understanding of the Holocaust. How dare I selfishly exploit this man's pain as a teaching tool?

But to my surprise, Adolf quietly said: "You know, I talked with my wife last night. If you think the kids will understand, then I will come to talk to them. There's more than Anne Frank to the Holocaust. Tell them about me. Have them prepare questions."

We set a date, and I told the children about Adolf. They were excited about meeting someone who had been a child during the Holocaust and who had survived. As one of the students put it: "Adolf can talk to us. We can ask the questions we have about Anne, and he can answer for her."

Although I quickly reminded the students that Adolf's experiences in Romania were different from Anne's, they were right that he was a child who had lived to share these times.

A subdued Adolf came into my classroom with his treasured photographs. He sat down, and the students began asking him questions. At first, he answered in a soft voice. But then he looked at the group of thirty multiethnic children and opened up to them: He passed around his photos and began to tell of his fears as a child. In response to the students' questions about the food served at the camp (a carryover from our nutrition unit), Adolf graphically told them what was eaten to maintain life. He told a harrowing story of his mother's being shot to death in front of him, when he was four.

I stood at the back of the room so Adolf could feel he was just alone with the children. Suddenly, I heard the sound of sobbing. Adolf was crying. Two of the children moved close to him. One went to get him water. The others sat in silence.

What had I done in the interests of education to a man who did not want to talk about the Holocaust and by his own admission had never cried about it? I felt guilty.

But then the sobbing stopped. Adolf regained his composure. He told the children he had never cried for his mother until this day, well over forty years after her death. He told the children that they must prevent the Holocaust from ever happening again. Despite the fact that they were not Jews, he reminded them that what had happened to the Jews as a minority group could happen to them as well. The students didn't need this reminder because some had experienced violence that had driven them and their families from their native homelands.

Adolf told the children how he became a tough problem child in post-Holocaust Romania. He told of still encountering anti-Semitism as one of the few Jews left in his town. As an adult and a father of two daughters, Adolf was able to understand his father's strictness with his only surviving child. Although Adolf had never been close or comfortable with his father, he told the children he now realized how deeply his father had loved him.

"Yes, he carried you on his shoulders out of the concentration camp to life," said one of the boys.

"He did, indeed," replied Adolf as tears filled his eyes.

Extensions of Reaching Out, Reaching In

After Adolf's visit, the students drew scenes from Adolf's life. Many wrote him notes. One dramatized the night his dad woke up the four-year-old to carry him to freedom. Another wrote a story about Adolf's school days when he would fight those who called him names. As the students noted, Adolf was a "real life" person from the Holocaust who could tell them how it was. They compared his experiences to those of other Holocaust victims—he had survived, while Anne had left a great diary but couldn't answer questions. Through their reflections and writings, the students assessed their own understandings of a tragic historical event and its relation to their own lives.

I worried about Adolf's reaction to the class and to his own long-repressed tears. As we left the classroom, Adolf hugged me. "Find me other classes to speak to. I feel better. I can talk to children. I must!"

My 6th graders and I had reached out to Adolf. I realized that not only had he added immeasurably to our understanding of his experiences, but we had helped him reach in to touch and heal his own pain. The children, Adolf, and I had participated in the most integral component of learning: personal sharing. There was no question: All of us were the better for it.

A postscript: Adolf did talk to children in many other classes, and he requested that his real name be used in accounts of his experiences.

Strategy 6.
F.A.L.L. Into Literature

Following Through First Lines of Literature

As a lover of literature and a lifelong writer, I always try to find ways to draw my middle school students into reading and writing. Initially, I tried separate sets of strategies to motivate them to do independent reading and to develop a love of creative writing. But one strategy, inspired by a "gimmick" book, performed a dual service as a catalyst for both reading and writing. This strategy is called "F.A.L.L. Into Literature"—a first- and last-lines (F.A.L.L.) approach to reading and writing.

First lines first: When I was going through the bargain bookshelves at a bookstore in search of an appropriate prize for the winners of a citywide writing contest, I found an enthralling title: *In the Beginning—Great First Lines From Your Favorite Books* (collected by Hans Baven, San Francisco: Chronicle Books, 1991). I bought enough copies of the book for all the winners.

While I was inscribing the books, I leafed through the volume and picked out the first lines of many of my favorite works of literature. As I was going through the book, I realized that many of the first lines were evocative in and of themselves. Just for fun, I immediately began mentally continuing the plots suggested to me by the first lines from unfamiliar literary works. I pulled out my notebook and copied down the unfamiliar lines that particularly intrigued me. I also noted the titles of the books these lines were taken from, so that after I wrote out my continuations, I could read the works to see how the actual writers had developed their stories.

Then it hit me. Since these selected first lines had sparked me to do some creative writing and reading, why not try the same strategy with my middle school students? Because the students were less well read than I was, the potential number of unfamiliar first lines and hence opportunities for reading and writing were far greater for them than for an adult reader. But would they be intrigued by these first lines?

I selected several first lines from works I felt confident the students hadn't read, but whose reading would be an accessible and age-appropriate experience for my ethnically diverse, middle school students in New York City. They were:

1. "Serene was a word you could put to Brooklyn, New York."
2. "Early in the spring of 1750, in the village of Juffure, four days upriver from the coast of The Gambia, West Africa, a man-child was born to Omoro and Binta Kinte."
3. "Somewhere a child began to cry."
4. "Now she sits alone and remembers."
5. "The law, as quoted, lays down a fair conduct of life, and one not easy to follow."
6. "I look at myself in the mirror."
7. "José Palacios, his oldest servant, found him floating naked with his eyes open in the purifying waters of his bath and thought he had drowned."

I reproduced these on a "F.A.L.L. Into Literature—First Line Follow-Through" worksheet and distributed copies to the class (see Worksheet 5, "F.A.L.L. Into Literature," in Section III, Resources). The students were given a chance to read through the quotes and decide which ones particularly intrigued them or raised questions for them. When they had had a chance to review the first lines on their own, they shared their initial reactions. Among their comments were:

> That quote about Brooklyn must be from some really out-of-date book. *Serene . . .* are you kidding?

> Is Juffure a real place in Africa? I'm going to look it up.

> She sits alone and remembers . . . that's my grandma . . . she's always talking about what happened long ago.

> That José quote could be the opening of a detective story.

> Children are crying everywhere. Is that from a book about Bosnia?

As they talked, the students "sparked" writing ideas from one another's comments. They discussed which quotes were suggestive of mystery (#7) and of horror (#6 and #7). Also they speculated that quotes #1 and #2 were from stories in which geography played an important role.

After the students had shared their initial responses to these first lines, I invited them to build on the lines and author the first paragraph of the works quoted. The students were encouraged to choose those first lines they found most inspiring. They were given about 15 minutes to develop paragraphs that followed logically from these lines.

When the students finished their independent authoring, they shared their "First Line Follow Through" paragraphs. As the students read their work, I made no comments, but encouraged them to respond to one another's writings. Many students expressed support and admiration for each other's writing. Because only seven quotes had been offered on the initial worksheet, many of the students wrote "First Line Follow Throughs" to the same quote. They were fascinated by and appreciative of the multiplicity of logical follow throughs possible from different individuals for the identical first line.

The session ended with students asking me to reveal who the authors were and what books the first lines were from. I allowed the students to "coerce" me into revealing the identities of the first-line authors and their works:

1. Betty Smith, *A Tree Grows in Brooklyn*, 1943
2. Alex Haley, *Roots*, 1976
3. Elie Wiesel, *Dawn*, 1960
4. Carlos Fuentes, *The Old Gringo*, 1985
5. Rudyard Kipling, *The Man Who Would Be King*, 1888
6. James Baldwin, *If Beale Street Could Talk*, 1974
7. Gabriel Garcia Marquez, *The General in His Labyrinth*, 1989

My reward was watching the students copy down the sources of their favorite first lines and hearing them say they'd read the books.

Falling Back into Literature from Last Lines

Because the initial "First Line Follow Through" project was so successful—and enjoyable—I decided that the students might also respond to the challenge of "falling back" into literature by working backward in plot from the last lines of literary works. But this time, rather than create my own worksheet of last lines from literary works for them, I asked each of my students to select the last line from a favorite book and write it on a piece of paper. They were given two days and asked to select books whose last lines would not be easily identified by their peers.

When the students came to class with their selections on slips of paper, I distributed small envelopes to each student. I asked them to write their names on the front of the envelopes, place the slips inside them, and seal the envelopes. One student collected the envelopes and redistributed them so that no student got his own envelope back.

Next, the students opened their envelopes and wrote paragraphs to precede the last lines—"falling back" into the plots that preceded the lines. Once the students had written their "last" paragraphs, they shared them with the student whose name was on the envelope. The student then revealed how close to the actual last paragraph of the literary work the writing was. The students shared the titles and authors of their last lines with one another. They were eager to exchange works so they could read one another's author.

Benefits of the F.A.L.L. Into Literature Strategy

The "F.A.L.L. Into Literature" strategies were also used by my students as peer teaching and parent-child workshop strategies. The envelope approach proved particularly popular, because every student was both a preparer and a participant in the strategy. It also served as one type of student-developed assessment in the peer review process inherent in this strategy.

This easily infusible strategy focuses students on key aspects of classics and actively engages them in the authoring process.

As a consequence of this "collaboration" with the actual writer of a particular piece, students become accustomed to the roles of reading and writing *insiders*. Those are good roles to "F.A.L.L." into.

Strategy 7. Storyboarding Reader Response

A Strategy for Right-Brain Learners

With the increasing availability of videos, television, and arcade games, I find that drawing my junior high students into the circle of literate, engaged lovers of written texts is more challenging than ever. To add to the magnitude of this challenge, many of the children I teach in an inner-city, urban, middle school setting are what Madeline Hunter (1984) identifies as right-brain learners, either genetically or courtesy of the television set. For some of my students from homes where English is not the native language, visual learning is the optimal mode for teaching reading and writing because they do not have ready access to the cultural codes and English vocabulary skills necessary for more traditional approaches to the teaching of these skills.

By the time these right-brain learners come to my English classroom, they often sadly demonstrate the truth of Betty Edwards' (1989) observation: "The right brain learner—the dreamer, the artificer, the artist—is lost in our schools . . . and goes largely untaught (p. 37)." By introducing my students to the animator's tool—the storyboard to plot films and cartoons in sequenced panels—I have begun to teach these right-brain learners and myself the wonders of picturing the rich imagery in many texts. This strategy has not only been useful in my own multiethnic classroom. It also has benefited a network of peer middle school teachers who work in elementary schools, as well as my graduate students at Manhattanville College and Fordham University.

One evening, about two years ago, I glanced

This section is adapted from "Storyboard Exchange," in *Ideas Plus: A Collection of Practical Ideas, Book Seven* (Urbana, Ill.: National Council of Teachers of English, 1989). Copyright © 1989 by the National Council of Teachers of English. Adapted by permission.

up from my own writings to watch my husband, Steve, at work. Steve, a filmmaker who works with computer graphics, was creating a storyboard form for his computer graphics class to complete in their lab time as slide animations the next day. I grabbed the sheet from him and looked over its panels. Great! I knew my kids would go for this as a way of teaching sequence. "Maybe I can use this with my English classes," I said to my husband.

"Never!" Steve intoned in his usual dismay whenever I step out of my "language arts" territory into his "fine arts" terrain.

Of course, I introduced storyboarding with a class of my average multicultural 7th graders the next day. First I distributed the storyboard sheets (see Worksheet 6, "Storyboarding Reader Response," in Section III, Resources) and asked the students what it reminded them of. Many recognized it as a set of panels for a comic strip, and others suggested that each panel could be divided into two sections for the words or story and a picture above. Some saw in the format a photo essay or illustrated book, comic book style. None of the students in that first, average, inner-city school actually identified the storyboard sheet as the tool of the animator. However, in subsequent semesters—because of the popularity of the *Roger Rabbit* cartoon and TV programs detailing animation—many students were able to recognize the "fine arts" use of the storyboard. This recognition enhanced the seriousness and practicality of its use in my classes because the students knew that salaried professionals with art talent actually were highly regarded for their skills at storyboarding.

Introducing Storyboarding Through Cartoons

As training or a mini-lesson in the *sequencing* I wanted the students to demonstrate when they used this tool, I asked them to name their favorite cartoons. Then I asked for the typical plot or action involved in the cartoon. The students came up with Bugs Bunny, and we discussed how many different drawings each could come up with that would show progressive movement changes in the lifting of Bugs' arm as he prepares to nibble his carrot. Since I am always eating carrots anyway, I delighted in serving as the living model for my students' discovery of the infinite movements necessary to visually sequence this characteristic movement, which finishes with the Porky Pig voice-over: "Th-th-th-that's all, folks."

In subsequent semesters, I would often bring in the VCR and run a cartoon on it, using the pause and freeze-frame controls on the remote to demonstrate to students how many animations went into one fleeting motion/dialogue sequence. They were always astounded by the number of frames, especially when I let them write down their guesses beforehand and then compare them with the reality. Given the combination of my slowly lifting a carrot and the opportunity of viewing a cartoon several times to count frames, the students in my English class certainly didn't think they were studying anything remotely related to reading and writing, which were not their areas of past scholastic success, anyway.

Using Storyboarding with a Literary Selection

Then I lowered the proverbial boom. I distributed fresh, blank storyboard sheets and told my students they were going to use the sheets just as an animator would. But what story or action were they to animate? They would not have to sequence a story out of their imaginations (that might come later); but rather I would read aloud to them a section of a book we were studying as a class.

I chose to read aloud just the opening paragraph. I told the students that I would read aloud the opening paragraph three times very slowly. As I read, their task was to record in the storyboard panels, going from left to right, as many plot developments, mood changes, dialogue lines, and descriptive details as they

could capture. Because there were to be three readings, the students knew they could relax. If they missed certain details on one hearing, they could surely come up with them on the next hearing. I suggested that the students who wished to do so might actually "draw" the actions detailed in the text, while other students might opt to detail in their own words the sequences. I did not hand out copies of the printed text of the selection I chose—which was the opening of Ray Bradbury's *Fahrenheit 451*. Just before I began reading the first paragraph of the text, I asked the students to jot down their guesses as to how many pages of text it would take to fill a storyboard. Most guessed at least three pages.

I then read the opening paragraph of the text three times. Each time, my students looked a bit more assured as they carefully listened and captured on the panels the suggested plot, mood, dialogue, and descriptive elements I had set as their listening focus. By the time I finished the third reading, I could see that many of the students looked confident; but a few still seemed upset and lost. My not-so-hidden agenda for storyboarding was to animate and enchant my students as readers and as writers. Therefore, at this point, I handed out copies of the first printed page of *Fahrenheit 451* so that the students could now look at and—thrill of thrills—actually "read" for themselves the text I had been reading aloud. From listeners of the tale to independent readers, my novice storyboard animators reread the text. Several who had looked upset after the three readings now happily filled in the details they had missed. However, as a surprise to both the students and me, several students who had appeared pleased with their "captured" details from my reading raised their hands and sheepishly requested a second storyboard sheet—although none of them had thought that the content of the first paragraph of any story could fill a nine-box storyboard sheet.

I gave the students an additional 10 minutes to "work up" their storyboards as I went around, astounded by their attention to the printed text and the care they gave to what, in some cases, was their second, revised storyboard ("I want to do it over, Mrs. Reissman—I can do better").

After the students had completed their storyboards—and their independent revisions, in this case an actual "reseeing and redrawing"—I asked them to hold up their individual storyboards. The students and I examined the diverse collection of panels inspired by the same text. We all marveled at the degree of details and narrative complexity, albeit different ones for different readers and listeners, that the various class members had been able to extract from the text.

I then invited students who were particularly proud of their work to display their storyboards on the wall. Three students volunteered to do so; and one was "volunteered" by his peers, who were really impressed with his artwork. (This student, three years below grade level, had right-brain capacities that could obviously be far better used than his Spiderman doodles in his notebook suggested.) Another capable student, Cheng Duong, had been in the United States for only two years. She said that doing her storyboard helped her really picture the "hard English words"; and she took justifiable pride in her beautifully detailed storyboard. I later used it in teacher training workshops, many of which Cheng attended.

Extending Storyboarding Activities

As part of our next storyboarding section (the initial one used up the whole period, but the class literally didn't want to leave), the students viewed various "donated" (student permission given) storyboards that were placed around the room. They discussed the similarities and the differences between the sequences. My designated class recorder (a student with a legible board handwriting and patience neces-

sary to transcribe other students' comments) went to the board and listed the various kinds of images and key words evoked by the opening text of *Fahrenheit 451*. (Some students simply put key words or verbal concepts into the boxes because they felt their drawing skills were minimal or they didn't "see" pictures when they listened to or read a story.) Next, the students reviewed their initial guesses as to how many text pages would fill out a storyboard. They were surprised to find that a truly detailed pictorial or verbal breakdown of the novel's first paragraph had filled two storyboard panel sheets, and some even extended into a third sheet.

As a follow-up to this activity, I asked students to randomly select another *Fahrenheit 451* passage and storyboard it in text or pictures. Several students, some talented artists and readers and some who had never succeeded at English or "been into reading," asked if they could try this technique with works they had read on their own. These works included texts I wouldn't normally teach or share in my English reading and writing workshops, such as Harlequin Romances and wrestling magazines. But I agreed and also commissioned some students to storyboard newspaper stories. Among those student teams commissioned were students who read well and those who drew well but read below grade levels, according to standardized tests.

The products of these storyboard lab workshop sessions were rich in critical narrative details, properly sequenced, from varied texts, which the students attached to their efforts. (See Figure 3.1 for a sample student-created storyboard from *The Joy Luck Club* by Amy Tan.) Many students formed collaborative partnerships that produced aesthetically pleasing, visual renditions of both news events and literary classics. Some students, recognizing that this would be a wonderful technique to share in the various workshops I conducted, volunteered to storyboard various works for me and formed in-class animators' sections where they would happily

FIGURE 3.1
Sample Student-Created Storyboard

give up lunch to sit together and storyboard *Huckleberry Finn* or a children's poem I planned to share with elementary classes I visited.

Using Storyboarding with Peer Teachers

Many students in my middle school English classes are members of the Peer Teaching Corps, which works in the Writing Institute program in elementary schools across New York City. These peer teachers immediately asked if they could use storyboarding in peer teaching. They selected their own stories and poems that they thought appropriate and copied ample supplies of storyboards. As it turned out, all of P.S. 190, our "host" elementary school, was soon filled with storyboards, not only of tales the 4th graders were reading, but also of passages from their social studies books. The participating teachers requested even more of my students' time for storyboard instruction. The peer teachers delighted in teaching this reading and writing skill to the "little kids"—after all, they were mature 7th grade teaching professionals, while their students were only 3rd or 4th graders. One teacher who successfully used this technique with many of her classes observed:

> The 3rd graders think of it as a "fun" way of learning. In my opinion, storyboarding, whether used with the newspaper or books, helps people break down important events which happen in the story. It

also helps them to understand what they are reading.

Using Storyboarding with Advanced Students

In a class of advanced, above-grade-level 7th graders at Ditmas Junior High, I showed the students the first 5 minutes of Truffaut's film version of *Fahrenheit 451* and had the students storyboard the film version, using some of the guidelines offered by Bryan and Davis (1975, pp. 159–176). These advanced students approached this experiment with zest. As a result of prior practice with storyboarding, their initial storyboards of the film version were far more detailed, in both words and pictures, than their first text efforts. Once the film segment was completed, the students themselves initiated a discussion of the ways in which their film storyboards compared and contrasted with the actual text of the book. I then facilitated the students to suggest ways in which their storyboards could be used as visual notes for comparison-and-contrast essay formats.

When the students in this class actually referred to their storyboards as visual data for such essays, the supportive details in the paragraphs generated for the comparisons were superior in richness and quality of expression to other comparisons they had written. Several students spoke of "seeing" and then writing down the differences and similarities between the film and text versions of this modern classic.

I looked at the wonderful, "expert" storyboards these students created, as well as some of those culled from students who had artistic ability and were also in my peer teaching corps. Why not use some of these as story starters for other writers—both students and teachers in my workshops—who were not studying these particular pieces of literature with me? I duplicated several, including Cheng's *Fahrenheit 451* opening storyboard and distributed them to classes of middle school students and teachers attending my reading workshops. The groups were divided into teams of three or four students each, whose task was to "write out" the text that had inspired the particular storyboard. Various differing, written versions of the storyboards were presented. Then everyone was given the copy of the *Fahrenheit 451* passage that had inspired Cheng's storyboard. Many learners—teachers and students alike—really enjoyed discovering how their storyboards matched up with Bradbury's actual words. Some 7th graders and several colleagues felt they had composed better stories than Bradbury's.

Using Storyboarding with Special Education Students

I introduced storyboarding on an experimental basis to students in P.S. 190's special education classes for 10–11-year-olds with language impairments, who had been studying media versions of classics.

I read the kids the opening of Antoine de Saint-Exupery's (1971) *The Little Prince* three times, and then their teacher and I asked them to storyboard it. Then we viewed a National Education Association (NEA) video version of *The Little Prince*, and the students storyboarded that as well. These students with language impairments really took to storyboarding; in fact, their teacher reported to me that, in addition to their weekly sessions with me, the students voluntarily storyboarded other stories and films.

I later trained special education teachers in my district (District 25), as well as District 20 in Brooklyn. Another of our cooperating classroom teachers in the peer teaching program, an expert English-as-a-second-language (ESL) teacher on the junior high level, was so impressed with the work of my 7th grade peer teachers, Lynda Chin and Cheng Duong, that she adapted their storyboarding techniques and incorporated them into her ESL lessons. She used storyboarding with 12- and 13-year-olds to help them begin writing, drawing, and sharing the stories of their arrival in the United States as part of her "This Is My Country" project. Her ESL students also used storyboards to enhance, through art, their English-literacy ability as they shared memories of their native homelands and sites of their new Brooklyn neighborhood. This teacher noted:

> For these new arrivals to the strange world of Brooklyn and Ditmas Junior High 62, storyboarding made sharing stories of all kinds and reading/writing about written texts a "guaranteed success," which is so important for future accomplishments in the acquisition of reading and writing skills.

Benefits of Storyboarding

One student, Kala Mandrake, a fine artist as well as an avid, above-grade-level reader, embraced storyboarding because it helped her "see and understand what was actually going on in the book much better than just reading it and answering questions." She noted that in preparing her storyboards, she had to make creative decisions "involving design, plot, and events just like the author of the text had to."

Confirming comments by Donald Graves (1984) that "writing is a kind of photography with words," (p. 73), several of my students who were home video buffs or camera enthusiasts did very well with the assignment. They shared with the class insights from their work in planning "shots" for a media project and how these skills transferred to their text storyboarding. This activity was an example of the many kinds of authentic, student-developed assessments that occurred continuously throughout the project.

Six years into "storyboarding," I routinely infuse the technique into my standard reading and workshop activities for both adult teachers and children. I keep a ready supply of at least 100 blank storyboard sheets, which I am continually replenishing. Readers and writers of all ages happily vie with one another to see how many distinctive panels they can generate from a common given passage. Many students who once doodled in English class and still do in other classes—given the evidence of their notebooks (or, shall we say, unauthorized sketch pads with interspersed subject notes)—are now using their right-brain learning abilities to succeed in making texts "live," to the applause of their peers. As they do so, storyboarding is helping them develop an "integrated learning style" (Hunter 1984, p. 39), which can be crucial for their future reading and writing successes.

Since I invaded the animator's territory and seized storyboarding as a reading and writing tool, my students—both teachers and schoolchildren—and I have been conquered by its power to make us see, share, sequence, detail, and compare various verbal, written, and visual texts. We invite you to explore the infinite uses of storyboarding for animating reading and writing workshops.

Strategy 8. Cresting for Character and Community

This strategy uses the concept of family crests to explore cultural values of various works of literature. Students work cooperatively in groups that encourage the use of multiple intelligences, particularly spatial and interpersonal intelligences.

Introducing Cresting

One day as I stood transfixed in front of a toy store display of plastic, miniature Marvel figures, I overheard a child say: "I really like that shield—look at how it shows the spider!" Both the child and I wound up in line to buy the figure: he for its "neat" flashing spider and

---

This section is adapted from "Cresting for Character and Community, in *Ideas for the Working Classroom: Classroom Practices in Teaching English*, Vol. 27, Kent Gill, editor, and the Committee on Classroom Practices (Urbana, Ill.: National Council of Teachers of English, 1993). Copyright © 1993 by the National Council of Teachers of English. Adapted by permission.

I for its "crest," which I saw as a motivator for my "Cresting for Character and Community" unit.

The child's enthusiasm crystallized for me a means of achieving a key *affective* goal I had decided to incorporate into my language arts curriculum—development of students' self-esteem and community involvement through use of visual imagery, reflection, critical thinking, writing, and oral communication. My Spiderman figurine served as a starter for a three-lesson module of activities, which I piloted in 1993. The project was successful: it received great student "customer" acclaim and more than satisfied the goal I had set.

I introduced the project during the first period of the module by handing out and displaying various duplicated shield/crest patterns I had culled from encyclopedias. In addition, my Spiderman figurine journeyed up and down the rows of my 7th grade inner-city classroom. I directed the students to select one of the duplicated shield patterns or crest copies or the Spiderman figure. Once they had selected one of these models to focus on, I asked them to try to decide what kind of personality or values were reflected in this model. I gave the students 3 minutes to independently reflect on the personality or values (I defined these as "what was important to") of the shield/crest bearers.

Following the 3 minutes of independent reflection, we shared the students' insights as to the personalities and values. I requested that for each value or personality trait they cited, they make reference to a particular visual component of the shield. Then I distributed various British monarch crests and African tribal emblems. I had the students suggest what these families and tribes valued given the evidence of their shield/crest emblems.

Next, I asked the students to take a few moments to jot down their own ethnic/cultural/religious identity, likes/dislikes (personal/cultural), favorites (foods/movie stars), and hopes for the future or dreams. After they had

sufficient time to do so, I told them to head this list up as a "crest inventory." Next I asked for two volunteers who would put up their inventories on the board. The rest of the class suggested appropriate visual emblems to match the inventory contents.

Finally, I distributed blank crest forms (see "Cresting Forms" in Worksheet 7 of Section III). The students' next task was to begin to design their own family shield, drawing visual emblems on their crests. I told them they could include the inventories plus any family memorabilia they could think of (i.e., flags of native lands, photos, stamps, post cards, etc.). Many students took the crests home to finish them.

During Period 2 of this module, my students exchanged the crests with one another. Each then "read" another student's crests. They told the crest designers what values or personality the crest suggested to them as observers. The student crest designers thus got immediate feedback on the success of their crest designs in communicating their crest inventories of values and traits.

After the initial shared "reading" of one another's crests, the class as a group discussed the difficulties in comprehending the crests, based on their inventory lists. We then brainstormed ways in which they could solve some of their common design problems. As another form of "cresting" that would be easier both emotionally as well as cognitively on students from troubled backgrounds, with poor self-image, I suggested the alternative of designing a crest for a friend or neighbor or for a popular TV/movie character.

Our culminating, Period 3 activity was a "What's My Crest?" version of the old "What's My Line?" TV show. Various crests were shared, with the peer audience either identifying family traits or depicting fictional TV/movie characters. Through the device of the show format, we "tested" the effectiveness of the class's crest design in communicating their identities or those of designated fictional characters to an audience. Many of the crests were selected for a hall exhibit. Several students who were also involved in computer graphics used a drawing program to create a slide show and printouts of the crests, as well. These activities formed part on an ongoing peer review of the "Cresting" project—assessments that we all enjoyed.

I hope to field test this project with ESL students—and I plan to ask my corps of 7th grade peer teachers to assist. Some of these first-time "cresters" tried it out in their peer teaching classes as a one-lesson project and were delighted with the results.

Go on your own "Crests" (quests) for community and character—your students will be all the richer for it, as both thinkers and individuals.

Extending Cresting Activities

Students can use the crest tool and the "common" and "culture specific" activities to prepare multicultural literacy anthologies based on their own readings. For example, in my classes I have used "Cresting" activities with *The Joy Luck Club* by Amy Tan (1989). (See Figure 3.2 for a sample student-created crest.) As a text for this activity (for upper elementary and secondary students), I used the opening paragraphs of this work, where the Chinese mother reflects on her hopes for her American daughter. The students shared their ideas, designed crests, and produced them through word-processing and computer drawing programs (see "Crests" forms and "Teachers' Instructions" in Worksheet 7, Section III, Resources).

FIGURE 3.2
Sample Student-Created Crest

In the instance of *The Joy Luck Club*, several students found the problems of communication, loss of native-language fluency, woman's status, and an inability to speak in "American English" common to their own backgrounds. Charlie Santangelo told of the way his Italian grandmother and great aunts were isolated and different from the American daughters. Janet Hur told of her mother's frequently articulated hope that her daughter would have her own "identity" beyond that of her husband. Joaquin Ortez said that his grandmother of 43, who had emigrated from Puerto Rico when she was 6 years old and spoke fluent English, was still "very different" from him and her other grandchildren. Elaine Lee said her Korean grandmother and her mother rarely spoke. Sometimes her mother would say to her grandmother: "Speak English to Elaine!"

Students also identified some of the "culture-specific" values found in the crests. In the selection from *The Joy Luck Club*, students identified the "Chinese" culture components of the text as: measurement of the wife by her husband's belch, the Shanghai market vendor's boast about the duck, and the "swallowing of my sorrow." Although students Aimee Chan and Grace Lee confirmed that these were indeed aspects of their family's Chinese backgrounds, several other students noted that similar metaphors and customs operated in their own cultures, which were Korean and Italian.

Other Sources of Cresting Activities

The following are some of the other selections I've used with upper elementary-secondary students (many of these suggestions came from the students themselves):

- Toni Morrison's *Beloved* (New York: Knopf, 1987) and The Bluest Eye (New York: Knopf, 1979)
- John Steinbeck's *The Pearl* [in the Lass second edition of 21 Great Stories (New York: Mentor, 1969)]
- John Hersey's *Hiroshima* (New York: Knopf, 1985)

- *I Never Saw Another Butterfly—Children's Drawings and Poems from the Terezin Concentration Cam*p, 1942–44 (New York: Schocken Books, 1978)
- Virginia Hamilton's *In the Beginning* (New York: Harcourt Brace, 1988).

Teachers who wish to develop classroom collections of multicultural literature appropriate for integration into their grade or themed curriculum should consult Carmen Farina's *Making Connections—A Multicultural Core Curriculum*—(1989), an annotated bibliography available from the New York City Board of Education, 110 Livingston Street, Brooklyn, New York 11201, or contact Ms. Farina directly at P.S. 6, 45 East 81st Street, New York, NY 10028. (See Section III, "Literature and Other Resources," for other bibliographies and anthologies of multicultural literature.)

Strategy 9.
Leaving Out to Pull In

Using Cultural Reader Responses to Teach Multicultural Literature

One day, as I was reading through a work of literature in the *Braided Lives* multicultural anthology (Appleman and Reed 1991), in which the author's name did not include her culture, I realized—when she finally explicitly stated her cultural background—that I had mistakenly assumed her culture was the same as mine. When I reflected on what contextual clues had led to this mistaken assumption on my part, I realized that I myself had *projected* my own cultural background and experiences of discrimination as a Jew onto this work. Although the author, Audre Lorde, was writing about a West Indian's experiences in Harlem (*Zami: A New Spelling of*

This section is adapted from "Leaving Out to Pull In: Using Reader Response to Teach Multicultural Literature," *English Journal*, February 1994. Copyright © 1994 by the National Council of Teachers of English. Adapted by permission.

My Name, pp. 186–190), I was not "wrong" in identifying parallel community reactions to myself as the lone Jew in some southern U.S. geographic settings.

I realized that my inaccurate, but empathetically appropriate, response to this reminiscence of a West Indian's childhood in Harlem, was a demonstration of a multicultural aspect of Louise Rosenblatt's (1978) reader response theory. Often this theory is used to explain why students comprehend or don't comprehend a particular narrative. I decided to use my own experience with cultural reader response to infuse multicultural understandings into my middle school (Grade 6) literature studies. My ethnically diverse students, the majority of whom were reading on grade level but were from non-native-English-speaking homes, and I evolved a strategy that grew out of their cultural reader responses to literature. The strategy is "Leaving Out to Pull In."

First, I told the students that they would listen to an excerpt from a work they had not previously read (*unfamiliarity with the work to be shared is essential for this exercise*). I assured them that I would read the excerpt aloud three times (to allow time for all to absorb its contents). I asked that during the readings they should try to guess the ethnic or cultural background of the author and write down the phrases, images, or words that suggested a particular ethnicity or cultural background to them. I told them that I would purposely "leave out" specific references or names of places, native language terms, or customs that would reveal the author's actual cultural background.

Next the students sat or reclined in their seats and listened to the passage, as I read it aloud the three times promised. I have used this technique to introduce three contemporary multicultural literature pieces: Amy Tan's *The Joy Luck Club*, Nicholasa Mohr's *Felita*, and Langston Hughes's "Theme for English B" (a poem). [*Note:* If you have used any of these works for one of the other strategies in this

book, such as the "Cresting" strategy, choose another multicultural work for "Leaving Out."]

"Leaving Out" with **The Joy Luck Club**. The excerpt I used from The *Joy Luck Club* is the introductory passage (pp. 3–4), where the old woman reflects on her immigration to America and her aspirations for her American-born daughter. Although the passage contains site- and Chinese-language-specific references ("Shanghai," "li"), these are left out and read as "blank."

When the three oral readings of this passage were concluded, I asked my ethnically diverse 6th graders, the majority of whom were Latino and black American, with one Korean student, what they felt the author's ethnic background was. I also asked them what country the old woman had been born in. These two questions were really targeted toward engaging the students in discussing the cultural hints they had gleaned from the reading.

My Korean student said he was certain the country was Korea. I had surely left out a town name, and the open-air market had to be Korea because his aunt talked of buying food in an open-air market.

One of the students thought the old woman came from Cuba because her own grandmother was "just like that." When I asked my student Maria what she meant by "just like that," she said that although her grandmother spoke only broken English, she kept urging Maria to speak only "American English" at home.

Carmen said that the lack of communication between the old woman and her American-born daughter was just like that between her own mother and her Puerto Rican-born great aunt and that surely this story had been written by a Puerto Rican.

But Darius, a black-American student, took exception to that comment: "What makes this a Puerto Rican story? My mother and my grandmother don't get along too well, even though they were born in the Bronx. And my uncle sometimes practices a big belch."

"Belching is an Italian custom. We have two neighbors who are Italian and do that. The writer must be Italian," said Racquel.

"No, this story sounds like a Japanese tale. 'Foolish Sum' . . . 'creature that become more than what was hoped for' . . . 'only one swan feather for a memory' . . . 'it comes from afar' . . . 'all my good attentions' . . . I copied down what you read. All of this stuff is like a Japanese design," argued Enrique.

"I took down the 'Foolish Sum' stuff and the 'swan feather,' too. But remember the swans in those Hans Christian Andersen fairy tales and 'the ocean'—to me these clues suggest a writer from Poland or Germany. They used to 'come across on boats' and enter at Ellis Island. I wrote Ellis Island down," said Marisol.

"I don't know what country the old woman is from, but I drew an Indian lady in a sari having her swan pulled out of her hands. The sari makes her very different from regular Americans," said Elvia.

When I told the students that I had left out the words "Shanghai" and "li" and that Amy Tan was a Chinese-American writer, they were initially a bit taken back. No one had guessed "right." But then they started to recover:

> Well, maybe Amy Tan is Chinese American and the old woman is also Chinese, but my grandma is still just like her with her "speak American English" all the time.

> Like I said, mothers and daughters often can't get along, even if they're both from the same place.

I asked the students what they thought of this "Leaving Out" game. They said "leaving out" had "thrown" them off the "right" cultural track. "But we brought in so much of our families and cultures, and what we said about them was true, too," said Elvia.

"Even though my family is Korean and I thought the open air was a clue to Korea, I still want to know the rest of the story. I still understand something about the old woman," said Harry.

"She still reminds me of my great aunt. I want to find out what's in her heart," said Carmen.

By their eagerness to plunge into the story to which they had "pulled in" their own cultural reader responses, my students verified the potential efficacy of the "Leaving Out to Pull In" strategy.

***"Leaving Out" with* Felita**. In addition to piloting this strategy with the Amy Tan work and a diverse 6th grade class, I tried it out in a school whose students were predominantly of Asian origin (Chinese), with a minority of black-American students. The class was a 5th grade class in a public school on Manhattan's Lower East Side. The work I used with this group was purposely from an author who described another culture, other than the predominant Chinese neighborhood one: Nicholasa Mohr's *Felita* (1979).

For the purposes of engaging my students in the concerns of this powerful story of a young Puerto Rican's schoolgirl's neighborhood move, I chose a selection from the "Trouble" chapter (pp. 33–35). In this chapter, Felita has moved to the new, "better" neighborhood where she and her family are a minority. Her mother has urged her to go out and play. She does so and quickly makes two new friends, Katherine and Mary Beth. But when Mary Beth's mother sees her on the street with her daughter and the other Caucasian girls, she calls the children away from Felita. As Felita passes them, Mary Beth and Thelma taunt her with comments like: "Why don't you stay with your own kind?" . . . "Can't you answer? No speak the English no more?" . . . "so many colors in your family . . . they ain't white . . . just trying to pass."

When I read this work I left out the specific colors cited ("Her mother is black and her father is white"). After this reading, there was a nervous silence. This in and of itself was an unusual reaction for my class. I asked them, in addition to guessing the cultural identity of the author, to tell me what their "gut" reaction to the excerpt was. The responses I got to this question were real eye openers.

Several of the students focused not on the character of Felita (whose culturally revealing name had been left out) but on the unnamed mother of Mary Beth, who had pulled the neighborhood girls away from her.

My mother . . . doesn't like me to be friends with anyone who isn't Chinese. That's what hit me. But I have some Black and Cuban friends, although my mother doesn't know about them.

My grandfather once told us that we need to stay within our neighborhood. I wasn't sent to the new Magnet Computer school because it takes "all kinds," not only Chinese. Even if I make Stuyvesant H.S., (a special high school) I don't know if I'll be allowed to go.

I want to go to the Upper Lab (a junior high school for gifted and talented students), but my father won't even go to the open house because it's not a "Chinese" school.

I have seen Chinese mothers pull their kids away from me. As a black in this school, I feel like the girl in the new neighborhood. This book was done by a black brother, yes?

"Stay with your own kind." . . . We live in this neighborhood (Chinatown) because that's where my mom was able to get a rent she could make. But she hears that all the time. . . . Even the other Moms don't have much to do with her. Not because she ain't white, but because she's Puerto Rican.

The students were surprised to find that Felita was a Puerto Rican girl and that Mary Beth's mother was a biased Caucasian, a "white woman."

I'm surprised—I was sure she was Chinese. Guess this shows not only Chinese are like this.

After this discussion, the students wrote about incidents in their own lives, where they had been warned against or pulled away from peers of another ethnicity. Although all students wrote on this topic, only five of them shared these pieces aloud, at their own request. As the facilitator of this literary experience, I noted that the strategy had motivated the majority of middle school students from Chinese backgrounds to identify with the situation and characters portrayed in *Felita*. In their initial response to the excerpted passage—with its anonymous references to parent-imposed barriers to friendship with peers from other ethnic backgrounds—my students' openness, awareness, and eagerness to examine this cultural-bias issue surprised all of us. The technique had social value in that it *focused the students on their own power to reduce the effects of prejudice and bias.*

"*Leaving Out*" with "Theme for English B." When I did a presentation for a parochial school group in Wilmington, Delaware, which had a homogeneous 7th grade student population with students from lower-middle-class, Caucasian, Catholic backgrounds, I decided to try out another selection from the *Braided Lives* anthology (Appleman and Reed 1991)— Langston Hughes' poem "Theme for English B" (pp. 210–211). In this poem, Langston Hughes reminisces about his New York City college days as a 22-year-old black youth from Winston Salem who is asked to write a "page" out of his own experience as a theme assignment.

For this demonstration lesson, I read aloud the whole text of this poem but left out culture-specific references and references to Harlem. I was eager to see what this homogeneous Caucasian parochial school audience would make of this poem. Their responses again confirmed reader response theory:

The "I" is from Northern Ireland. He sounds like my grandfather. He's always trying to tell us about what it is like to be a Catholic in Ireland.

The student sounds like this guy who works in my brother's garage. He's from Atlanta, Georgia, and keeps talking about himself as a southern boy. According to him, southern boys are polite, easy going, loyal, and fun to be with. This guy hangs out with my brother. He's been in Delaware a few years, but he still sees himself as a country boy from Atlanta.

The words "being _____ doesn't make me not like the same things other folks like who are other _____". . . "You don't want to be a part of me" . . . "I learn from you,/I guess you learn from me" . . . All of this spells "Jew" to me. Jews have this thing about being different and teaching and learning. My parents know a couple who are Jews. They say things like this.

The "I" is a Mexican. That discussion of eating, sleeping, drinking, and being in love says "Mexican" to me. I can't explain why.

It's somebody who came over at 10 from Korea or China and still feels like an outsider even at 22. But he has a sense of pride in who he is anyway.

The "I" is a black man in an all-white class. He belongs, but still knows he isn't white.

With the exception of the one boy who "got" the correct identity, the rest of the class were surprised by the fact that the student in the poem was black. But their discussion revolved around their empathy with being the only individual of a particular race or color in a class. One student shared his culture shock at visiting his cousin's class in Dade County, Florida, and being one of only three white students in a class of Latinos. Another student shyly told us about being frightened by all the "different" types of people she saw on 42nd Street in New York when she went to the theater.

I don't think of blacks as poets. I only see them as singers and sports jocks. This

Langston Hughes is really up front. He tells it like it is!

Although I visited that class only once, I felt the technique had served to broaden the students' appreciation of various ethnic groups and to highlight the commonality of cultural feelings when one is in the minority. In making comparisons and contrasts through their discussions and writings, the students engage in an ongoing assessment of their increasing cultural understandings.

I intend to continue using the "Leaving Out To Pull In" technique to engage student cultural reader responses to multicultural literature. The technique can serve as a tool for engaging and motivating students not only to probe the particular cultural backgrounds of the authors whose works are examined, but also to "pull in" their own cultural experiences to their reading. Such interactive reading will not only enhance literacy but also promote empathy and intergroup respect.

Strategy 10.
Showing Peer Portraits

Using "Peer Portraits" at the Beginning of the School Year

This strategy actually could precede all the others, because it is a good one to use at the beginning of the year, to introduce students to each other and to the teacher. By making portraits of their peers, students use multiple intelligences, such as spatial, intrapersonal, and interpersonal. The portraits—both written and graphic—make a superb mosaic to display around the room, or to place in a common area in the school.

I was introduced to "Peer Portraits" by a teacher who visited my class from South Jamaica, Queens, New York. This teacher has used "Peer Portraits" with junior high, ESL, and adult students. Though she had conceived of the project as part of an art curriculum (and with students who were having trouble being successful in school), she said she quickly realized how well it supported multicultural education, whole language, and motivation to learn.

"Peer Portraits" are limited only by your imagination—and that of your students. For example, I often ask my students to write "Acrostic Poems," such as the following:

Nancy is Italian
American Catholic
New York
Camaro sports car
Young woman's greatest love is her
family

The poems can be about their peers, teachers, family members, or themselves.

Other peer portraits can be drawn, either by computer graphics software or by hand, placed on paper "tiles," and displayed in the classroom. Students may choose to make cartoon bubbles showing a characteristic saying of the person drawn. Or they may choose to provide only the bubble and let the other students guess who is saying it. (See the "Peer Portrait" worksheets in Section III, Worksheets 8–10, for other suggestions.)

Using "Peer Portraits" with Literature

Many students enjoy making portraits of literary characters. The activities shown in the "Peer Portrait" worksheets can easily be modified to help students chart character development and to interest other class members in a particular book or story.

For example, using the "inverted literary technique," students may write a letter to a friend describing the character they have just "met." Students may be intrigued by writing a personal ad—"in search of"—as if the literary character were writing it. Or students could invent guessing games by writing three quotes from a character and asking classmates to identify the character (a type of student-developed

assessment). Other students may enjoy making trading cards featuring literary characters (see the "First Ladies in Profile" trading card strategy in Chapter 4).

Strategy 11. Atlas Cards

As I began to prepare learning center materials for a 6th grade newspaper-supported geography unit (see Chapter 4 for other newspaper-related strategies and activities), I was struck by the number and types of maps that were included in daily newspapers. I began clipping them out and pasting them on large index cards with the map on the front of the card and the accompanying news story (sometimes reduced by a copy machine) on the back of the card. Among the various kinds of maps I collected within just one week were: local road maps, national weather maps, metropolitan area maps, New York and Oklahoma state maps, national maps of Japan and Australia, a shoreline map of the Barnegat Bay estuary, New York City school district maps, a map of Cutler Ridge Mall in New Jersey, a map of Barcelona, a map of Oslo, and a map of Alaska's Kodiak Island.

I was also struck by the language arts applications of this project, and I decided to let my students in on the cutting and pasting and writing.

Atlas Cards—Newspaper Map Anticipation

I began my "Atlas Cards" language arts unit by dividing the students into teams of three or four students each. These teams were asked to estimate the number and type of maps they would find in that day's newspaper. They were also asked to decide what sections of the newspaper would contain maps.

After the students had worked together on these predictions, they shared their findings with the whole class. Only one of nine teams predicted more than five maps in a given daily newspaper. Most teams felt that any maps included in the newspaper would be in the first few pages in the world news sections. I made no comments about these predictions, but asked the students to post their predictions in paragraph form on the wall.

Next, I gave each student team three or four different daily newspapers, scissors, index cards, and glue. Since the students were multiethnic, some newspapers were foreign-language dailies. The students took 30 minutes to go through the newspapers to clip out relevant maps and the articles or captions accompanying them. They were asked to paste the maps on the front of the card and the articles or captions that detailed them on the back of the card. Just as I had done with my original cards, some of their articles needed to be reduced on the main office copy machine.

To the students' surprise, they discovered that they needed more than the available 30 minutes for creating their "Atlas Cards." They protested: "We've got too many maps."

The activity was continued the following day. As the students finished up their cards, I asked them to look at the posted paragraphs where they had made predictions about the number, types of maps, and the sections where they would be found. They then revised their predictions, in paragraph form, to reflect their actual, single-day map findings.

The students read their paragraphs aloud and then added their spontaneous comments about how surprised they were at the number and range of maps and the sections of newspapers where the maps were found. I shared with the students my own surprise when I had developed the "Atlas Card" prototypes in preparation for the unit. They suggested we use Sunday Travel sections and the travel ads in the newspaper. We marked off the diverse locations, regions, and places—three key geography themes that were the focus of our social studies unit.

Persuasive Argumentation/Writing—Atlas Approach

I asked the students whether putting together "Atlas Cards" from daily newspapers was a waste of time—after all, there were expensive atlas reference books in our library, and atlases could be bought in a bookstore, as well.

The students spent a class period talking together in their groups about this question. Then I asked them to write individual essays pro/con developing "Atlas Cards." The students then shared their persuasive essays with the whole class two days later (the students were allowed to "fix up" their essays at home).

Some students opted for use of a home or school library atlas, but many of the class members noticed that the maps published in the newspapers reflected political and social "reshaping" changes taking place each day, which could not be shown in an atlas. For example, one student noticed that even the most recently published atlas did not yet fully reflect the changes in Russian geography.

Mapping Questions and Answers—Student Talk Time

For the next activity—a student-developed assessment—we pooled our class-developed "Atlas Cards." They were all collected and then redistributed throughout the class so that students received cards that they had not compiled. I asked the students to develop at least three questions that could be answered by using the map. In addition, I distributed blank index cards for the students' use in writing the correct answers to the questions they developed.

While the students were developing their questions and answers, I went around the room to check if the questions were appropriate for the maps and if the answers were indeed correct.

The students then exchanged their "Question and Answer Atlas Cards." They enjoyed reviewing one another's questions and checking out the answers.

Map-Worthy Manifestos

The next activity also involved a writing project. The "Atlas Cards" were shuffled and re-distributed again, so that every 6th grader received an unfamiliar card. Then I challenged the students to examine the data on the card and decide why this map had been determined to be newsworthy. I suggested that after they made this decision, based on the data available, they should formulate their own opinion as to whether this story and the geographic themes it highlighted would continue to be in the news or would fade out within the week.

Because the students already had compiled their own "Atlas Cards" and reviewed cards created by other students, they had some background in the coverage of geographic themes. They enjoyed developing a point of view and judgment on the staying power of various stories. This activity also served as an assessment of how well students had processed the information they had learned, as well as an ongoing evaluation of their critical-thinking skills.

They not only wrote persuasive essays and editorials—"Map-Worthy Manifestos"—but also defended them orally in some heated discussions.

To provide students with a short-term opportunity to check and confirm the accuracy of the predictions in their "Map-Worthy Manifestos," each student stated what would happen to the coverage of that geographic area within a two-week span. By setting this brief span as a target, the students actually were able to review their predictions and examine how valid their predictions were. In addition, during the review, the students articulated the often unpredictable political, social, or climate factors that had literally knocked the map-worthy story out of the news.

At-Large Atlas Card Cartooning

As described earlier in this chapter, one of our regular literature study and writing activi-ties included storyboarding. In addition, using various syndicated comic strips, students wrote and drew imaginary preceding installments (we called these "prequels"), sequels, and con-tinuations, as well as commentaries on the car-toons. As we were developing these installments, in a project called "At-Large Lan-guage Applications," the students asked if they could put our "Atlas Card" facts into some of their cartoon-based creative writings. The fol-lowing are synopses of some of the projects:

- Gary Trudeau's "Doonesbury," with its focus on political and social issues, was one of the students' favorite choices for "At-Large Atlas Cartoon-ing." The "Doonesbury" characters took their readers to the Ramenshoye proletarian district where they peeked in on Russia's referendum on Boris Yeltsin's presidency.
- "Cathy" was interested in buying real estate in the Barnegat Bay area near Forked River, New Jersey.
- Tom and El in "For Better or For Worse" debated Community School District 25's election and analyzed the ethnically diverse population of Flush-ing, Queens.
- "Brenda Starr" and "Dick Tracy" were sent on separate missions to investi-gate a terrorist bomb that sprayed glass over streets around the 52-story NatWest Bank Tower, a London land-mark, and the Hong Kong, a Shanghai bank.
- Dagwood wandered around Miami's Cutler Ridge Mall to find Mervyn's, where he had to deliver a catering or-der for "Blondie."

The students took great pleasure in incorpo-rating elements of the "Atlas Card" maps and news data into these cartoons. Their story-boards were initially posted around the room. Later, we compiled all the cartooning efforts into a student publication, which we shared with the whole middle school.

At-Large Atlas Mystery and Travel Writings

The maps and detailed information about places, people, regions, locations, and movement within regions—the five geography themes—were a rich source of authentic data for the students to fold into two genres of writing, mystery and travel.

Some of the "Atlas Cards" were perfect for developing mystery stories. Among them was a map of the city of London, which was accompanied by the story, "London bomb blast kills 1, injures 34."

The students found that the map was a perfect, pictorial scene of the crime. They used it as the stage for detectives to collect evidence, identify suspects, and speculate on the planning of the crime and the escape route used by the perpetrators.

Many of the students had never traveled to or toured regions of the United States or other countries. Their travel readings, supplemented by selected passages from the writings of Ian Morris and Paul Theroux, inspired them to use the "Atlas Cards" as a source for their own wish-fulfillment travel writings.

Parents who had traveled extensively or did so as part of their jobs shared their experiences with us. Our "At-Large Atlas Cards" language applications project continues to grow as the students initiate design, writing, publishing, speaking, and outreach activities. Work with the burgeoning collection of newspaper-based "Atlas Cards" has promoted daily news reading by students and their families, as well as literacy with travel literature. The ongoing activities have also enhanced students' critical thinking, creative writing, expository writing, communication, interpersonal, and problem-solving skills.

The card collection offers an ongoing student-developed research resource that can continually be adapted to meet the needs of its student creators and the exigencies of current events.

❧   ❧   ❧

The next chapter describes trading cards, hero studies, newspaper collages, and other strategies that work well with social studies—but as with the "Atlas Cards," many of these activities are just as effective with language arts or with integrated curriculums.

References

Appleman, D., and M. Reed, eds. (1991). *Braided Lives: An Anthology of Multicultural American Writing*. St. Paul, Minn: Minnesota Humanities Commission.

Banks, J.A. (1988). *Multiethnic Education: Theory and Practice*. 2nd ed. Boston: Allyn and Bacon.

Banks, J.A. (1991). *Teaching Strategies for Ethnic Studies*. 5th ed. Boston: Allyn & Bacon.

Banks, J.A., and C.A. McGee Banks, eds. (1991). *Multicultural Education: Issues and Perspectives*. Boston: Allyn and Bacon.

Baven, H., ed. (1991). *In the Beginning—Great First Lines From Your Favorite Books*. San Francisco: Chronicle Books.

Bradbury, R. (1979). *Fahrenheit 451*. New York: Ballantine Books.

Bryan, M.B., and B.H. Davis. (1975). *Writing About Literature and Film*. New York: Harcourt Brace Jovanovich.

Edwards, B. (1989). *Drawing on the Right Side of the Brain*. Los Angeles: Jeremy P. Tarcher.

Gardner, H. (1983). *Frames of Mind*. New York: Basic Books.

Gardner, H. (1991). *The Unschooled Mind*. New York: Basic Books.

Gardner, H. (1993). *Multiple Intelligences*. New York: Basic Books.

Goodman, K. (1986). *What's Whole in Whole Language?* Portsmouth, N.H.: Heinemann.

Graves, D. (1984). *A Researcher Learns to Write: Selected Articles and Monographs*. Exeter, N.H.: Heinemann Educational Books.

Hunter, M. (1984). *Mastery Teaching*. El Segundo, Calif.: T.I.P.

Lockwood, A.T. (Summer 1992). "Education for Freedom." *Focus in Change* 7: 23–29. (National Center for Effective Schools Research & Development).

Mohr, N. (1979). *Felita*. New York: Baron, Skylark.

Nieto, S. (1992). *Affirming Diversity: The Sociopolitical Context of Multicultural Education*.

White Plains, N.Y.: Longman.

Rosenblatt, L. (1976). *Literature as Exploration.* 3rd ed. New York: Modern Language Association.

Rosenblatt, L. (1978). *The Reader, The Text, The Poem: The Transactional Theory of the Literary Work.* Carbondale: Southern Illinois University Press.

Routman, R. (1991). *Invitations.* Portsmouth, N.H.: Heinemann

Saint-Exupery, A. de. (1971). *The Little Prince.* New York: Harcourt Brace Jovanovich.

Tan, A. (1989). *The Joy Luck Club.* (Paperback ed.). New York: Bantam Books.

4 | Multicultural Social Studies

Because social studies are interdisciplinary, they are an excellent resource for helping students develop skills that will enable them to understand better and learn to interact effectively with other people. The instructional element of multicultural education must be integrated throughout the curriculum.

Gwendolyn Baker, *Planning and Organizing for Multicultural Instruction (1994, p. 322)*

Multicultural education is about uniting a deeply divided nation . . . a reform movement designed to bring about educational equity for all students. . . . It is caring, and taking action to make our society more just and humane. . . . A society is united within a framework of shared values, like democracy and equality.

James A. Banks, *Teaching Tolerance* (1992, p. 21)

Newspapers . . . become more necessary in proportion as men become more equal and individualism more to be feared. . . . They [newspapers] maintain civilization.

Alexis de Tocqueville (1831) (quoted in Olivanes 1993, p. v)

Teacher to Teacher

Teachers may have legitimate concerns about diluting the curriculum when other topics are infused into it:

Obviously, the very topic and themes of multicultural education are part of social studies. They can be a minicourse or an appropriate research project in an immigration or urban affairs course. But I don't understand how you can "infuse" multicultural understandings into aspects of social studies like geography, or what you should call literature/social studies— "socilit" units? Aren't you and other multicultural advocates stretching the scope of multiculturalism so thinly that it dilutes the legitimate language arts, history, and urban affairs concerns of this initiative?

But the goals of multicultural education are not limited to a "Band-Aid" multicultural lesson, course, or project. The goals of infusing the perspectives of multicultural education in "standard" social studies curriculums are goals that can be included in the teaching of basic social studies skills such as geography and historical research. For example, two strategies included in this chapter ("Geocurrents" and "Making Core Curriculum Connections") illustrate such an approach.

Well, sure, multicultural themes can be included in any content area, but why do they enhance instruction?

That's precisely the reason multicultural themes need to be included in geography and research projects. Through infusing the ethnic backgrounds of students into map, atlas, news, and general geography studies, we can contextualize these skills and tools for students and their parents as they relate them to their own backgrounds and experiences.

Benefits of Infusing Multicultural Perspectives into Social Studies

Life in Mexico or Leningrad becomes real to a student as he talks with a parent, community member, or peer who comes from or has lived in that country. Map skills acquire a context when a city or region is studied through family videos and photographs, with a narrative supplied by an "expert" adult who has traveled in the area. Beyond the geography text (which may well be outdated due to political changes), multiple perspectives on life, society, climate, and culture can provide authenticity to content. In addition, such active *social action* learning connects students to geography. Once a canon of fixed locations, facts, and boundaries, today's continually shifting geographic borders and realities can best be explored through a multicultural filter.

One of the strategies described here, "Newspapers in Education," is an especially effective multicultural classroom tool. By its very nature, the newspaper is the most up-to-date, if not unbiased, record of cultures, their current status, and their concerns (see the following "Cultural Collages" description). When students need to find out which groups have special interests, needs, or concerns, they can use newspapers as a living database to identify, analyze, and track these special needs groups (see the previously mentioned strategy, "Under the Multicultural Umbrella").

How better to engage students in Banks' (1991) social action approach than by having them identify human and civil rights concerns in the newspapers and use these authentic issues to devise their own legislation drafts and student-produced broadcasts on human rights issues? Why not use real-life issues to encourage lifelong learning and responsible citizenship? (see the "Newspapers" strategy "Responsibilities and Values").

If multicultural education goals are to engage students in studying common values, why not use newspaper-reported "heroes" as a catalyst for discussing what it means to be a hero? (See the "Newspapers" strategy "Hero Rites.")

Since the quintessence of multicultural education involves students and their families in ongoing cultural conversations, why not use daily newspaper reading as a basis for a dual-entry family journal (see "Family F.I.N.D." in Section III, "Worksheets," as well as "Mayoral Family F.I.N.D." in "Teaching Modules") that records family members' responses to the news? By maintaining this family journal with its cross-age perspectives, families can integrate the multicultural process into their lives and their reactions to community events.

Strategy 12. Geocurrents

Mapping and Mining the Multiple Intelligences Potential

Traditionally, geography, current events, and map content areas have engaged linguistic and mathematical learners. With our increasingly pluralistic, ethnically diverse population and ever-changing geographic currents, the traditional approaches to geography teaching, textbooks, atlas use, map study, and newspaper research can be expanded to include activities that are not only multicultural in approach, but also use students' multiple intelligences (Gardner 1983, 1991, 1993). Although the needs of linguistic and mathematical learners are usually met through existing traditional approaches, the needs of students with kinesthetic, auditory (musical), spatial, and highly developed interpersonal and intrapersonal intelligence capacities are often neglected.

Ethnically diverse, middle school students, a quarter of whom were from non-English-

This section is adapted from "International Currents Collage," *Notes Plus*, January 1993. Copyright © 1993 by the National Council of Teachers of English. Adapted by permission.

speaking homes, helped develop the "Geocurrents" strategy, with its emphasis on multiple intelligences. The students' creativity, use of the strategy in peer teaching, research activities, community outreach, and mastery of the five geography themes suggest that it has potential for broad dissemination.

Geocurrents Starter

"Geocurrents" begins with the class dividing into teams of two or three students each. I give the student teams two separate copies each of blank maps—outlines of the world and the United States. Students then meet together in their groups and predict the locations, places, and regions (three of the five geography themes) that will appear in that particular day's newspaper. I ask one student (the recorder) to list the locations, places, and regions predicted and ask another team member (the cartographer) to locate them on the maps. During this prediction time, the team is not allowed to consult an atlas or textbook for the correct map or the daily newspaper.

Once the teams have made their predictions, the team recorders and cartographers share them with the class as a whole. The group maps and list of locations, places, and regions can be posted in the room.

I then distribute the day's newspapers (at least one daily newspaper per team) and allow access to the atlas and updated world/U.S. maps. I give the students a chance to work collaboratively and cooperatively in their groups as they clip out relevant articles; list locations, places, and regions in the news; and accurately mark them off on the map.

Once the students have finished literally "cutting" through the newspaper, I give each team a chance to share their findings, and I encourage them to compare and contrast their actual findings with their own predictions.

Multiple Intelligence Aspects of This Initial Activity. In doing the "Geocurrents

Starter" activity, students have begun to mine the multiple intelligence potential inherent within geography study.

- *Linguistically* they have had to use reading and communication arts skills to identify relevant locations, places, and regions within the newspaper. As part of their team discussions, they have also had to use linguistic skills.
- *Spatial* skills have been integrated into the activity through the students' mapping of their findings. The actual display of the maps and lists also included spatial designs that reflected the teams' skills.
- *Logical-mathematical* intelligence was involved in estimating map site locations and distances, as well as predicting the number of sites. When these lists were checked against outcomes, a key aspect of problem solving was also involved.
- *Musical* intelligence, with all its auditory components, was involved in the team and whole-class discussions, as well as other oral expression. Actual musical performances evolved as follow-ups to this initial activity.
- *Interpersonal* exchanges were the channel for the teamwork and were also used within the group discussion. The teams responded to one another's lists.
- *Intrapersonal* conceptions of geography themes and newspaper coverage were tapped when the team members made their personal and team predictions before consulting the newspaper. When the teams compared their predictions with the outcomes of the activity, the individual students were also able to explore the way intrapersonal understandings permeated their predictions.
- *Kinesthetic* aspects of the activity included the actual cutting and clipping of the newspaper articles. In addition, several teams spread the newspapers out on the floor and sprawled down beside the papers. Groups moved around within their own spaces. The recorders and various students stood up when it was their time to speak.

Critical Thinking Core. In addition to engaging all seven multiple intelligences capacities, the "Geocurrents Starter" activity also provided students with a rich core of critical-thinking activities. Students worked with a given *problem construct*—how many and which locations, places, and regions are covered in a particular day's newspaper. They were asked to *make predictions* and *check outcomes*. They *checked* and *confirmed* these outcomes using the atlas, updated maps, and newspapers. They *compared and contrasted* each other's lists and maps. Students worked backwards and forward, using visual representations (maps) to develop verbal *questions* and *conclusions*. They *collected*, *synthesized*, and *analyzed data*. They *isolated* pertinent items.

Other activities in "Geocurrents" grew out of student initiatives and concerns. They can be used nonsequentially and adapted to meet the curricular needs of your class.

Newsmapping Geocurrents—A Collage

After they had already *clipped* and *cut* many geography-related headlines and stories, the students (their hands blackened with newsprint) wanted to make use of these clippings. I had a large wall-sized blank world map. A team of self-nominated "Geocurrents" designers collaged the headlines and some of these graphic clippings onto the map. They then put the rest of the articles into a file folder labeled with the date they were found and the newspaper used.

My class thought the map collage looked wonderful and was a great visual record of their findings. They asked if they could fill in another large world outline map when we used the newspapers again.

Not only did we make other collages on the large outline map, but I distributed additional individual world and U.S. outline maps to the students. They were then able to do their own "Geocurrents" map collages at home as individual research projects.

We were able to display the individual research collages and file folders in a student-designed and -run interactive Geocurrents Museum. Making the collages was extremely satisfying to the students. It also made their newspaper-based geography studies accessible to other students and parents.

This approach engaged the capacities of those who were spatial learners and also afforded those students with limited English-speaking skills a chance to fully participate in our research.

Musically Mapping and Parodying Our Georhythms

During our winter holiday celebrations, the students had easily learned how to include updated "Geocurrents" references to contemporary trends in holiday songs and advertising jingles. This activity had the added benefit of appealing to several of the multiple intelligences—linguistic, interpersonal, intrapersonal, and auditory (musical).

I challenged the students to apply this parodying skill to researching pop geography materials (such as travel brochures and ads for bargain trips), airline advertisements, musicals, and region-specific songs. Once they had identified songs, I asked that they conduct one of the following as a research project: get a copy of the lyrics and the date they were published; change, update, or parody these lyrics to meet "Geocurrents" findings; or get an audiotape or CD recording of the song to share.

The students not only brought in many classic musical standards (including music from *Zorba, Around the World in Eighty Days, Miss Saigon, Cabaret, 1776, Fiddler on the Roof*, etc.) but also shared foreign-language lyrics and audio recordings with multiethnic references to geography. Parents and community members came in to help teach us the songs.

Once the students had learned the songs in their native languages, they then changed some of the lyrics to reflect map changes or added verses of their own.

The climax of all this activity was a Geocurrents Musical Chorale songfest, which included students, parents, and community members. This celebration served as a culminating student product of this "Geocurrents" activity. The songfest not only accommodated auditory (musical), linguistic, interpersonal, and intrapersonal intelligences, but it also helped students focus on the geography themes of relationships, people, and places.

Geocurrents Newspaper Atlases— A Research Project

During the "Geocurrents" starter activity, the students discovered that the daily newspapers contained many maps of specific places, locations, and regions in the news. Some of these maps delineated another geography theme we were studying—movement of people within regions.

Over a period of four weeks, the student teams compiled their own "Geocurrents" news atlases as outcomes of newspaper-based research. For each map included in the atlas, the students noted the newspaper source and the date and wrote a summary telling why the map was included in the newspaper and how it tied into a current news issue.

As the atlases evolved, I provided the students with some background material on the five themes of geographic study suggested by the National Council of Geographic Studies: location, place, relationship of people within places, movement of groups, and regions. After we had reviewed these topics, I asked that students include brief explanations, if possible, in their map narratives of how these new maps addressed our geography themes.

Of course, the compilation of the atlases engaged the student teams in multiple intelligence activities—spatial, linguistic, mathematical, interpersonal, and intrapersonal. Student teams also wound up with *student-published* atlases that they donated to our library. As the students themselves noted, these were more up to date than the ones in the library.

Mathmapping—An Atlas-Based Math Problem Primer

The students were so proud of their atlases that they really didn't want to stop work on them, even after they were published.

One of my students who was in a citywide mathematics competition suddenly stood up in class and asked if her team could develop mathematics problems in scale, measurement, distance, and density, based on their maps.

"You know, we could run our own 'Geocurrents' math competition or do it as part of our interactive museum," suggested another student.

Although I am a language arts professional, I was delighted to let the students run their competitions. They authored companion pieces—books of "Mathmapping" problems—to go with the atlases.

In the Macintosh computer lab, we desktop published our atlases, scanned the maps from the newspaper, and published the "Mathmapping" primers. Using technology to further this initiative engaged the students' kinesthetic and spatial talents, as well as enhanced their interpersonal and logical-mathematical skills.

Geocurrents Composition and Commentary

As members of a language arts class, the students naturally reflected or wrote about and "linguistically" reacted to "Geocurrents" stories. For example, students have written papers persuasively arguing for and against U.S. intervention in Bosnia and Somalia. The Miami-Dade County Hurricane and the Great Storm of 1993 inspired poetry and reflections about beach erosion and flooding. Students wrote travelogues that included rich, vivid descriptions of faraway sites the students wanted to visit someday. These travelogues provided accurate background material for other travel-based literature, such as site-based mysteries.

Thanks to our Macintosh capacities, we were able to desktop publish these "Geocurrents" pieces as literature anthologies. Students read their pieces aloud at a publication party. These extensions engaged kinesthetic, auditory (musical), spatial, interpersonal, and intrapersonal student talents.

The "Geocurrents" multiple intelligences approach is still evolving, driven by middle-school student initiatives that reflect their diverse backgrounds and talents. The activities developed thus far represent "multiple entry points" (Gardner 1991, 1993)—through maps, collages (kinesthetic, spatial intelligences), music (musical-auditory intelligence), and museums and performances (interpersonal and intrapersonal intelligences; end products)—for exploring the five themes of geography. They all involve student-centered, cooperative, collaborative learning, which results in ongoing programs and projects that engage students, their families, and the community. As the boundaries and focuses of our "Geocurrents" project continue to flow, its directions have shifted according to public interest, current affairs, and community and student response. Multiple intelligence-supported methodologies serve to contextualize the five themes of geography study and to prepare students to be engaged citizens in this ever-changing world.

Strategy 13. Making Core Curriculum Connections

This strategy provides students and teachers with many ways to respond to what they are reading—and provides connections to a multitude of subject areas. Specific works of literature can be taught with activities that highlight geography, research, mathematics, values, science, semantics (or the more inclusive study of symbols, *semiotics*), and art. Section III includes two "Teaching Modules"—"Making Core Curriculum Connections" (1 and 2) that provide instructions for both students and teacher.

Worksheets are customized for two books: Nicholasa Mohr's *Felita* (1979) and Patricia Machachlan's *Sarah, Plain and Tall* (1985).

As mentioned previously, I have found Carmen Farina's *Making Connections* (1989) an invaluable resource for infusing multicultural perspectives in various areas of the curriculum. Figure 4.1 includes several quotations from Farina's work that can be handed out to students,

---

FIGURE 4.1

Making Multicultural Connections

It is essential in a multicultural environment that all children are expected to make an individual contribution to the learning environment (p. 9).

The teacher must include geography, writing, and most important, dialogue strands (p. 9).

Historical fiction allows us to personalize the social studies curriculum. . . . Teachers using historical fiction can integrate all curriculum areas, and in addition, cover skills, content, and concepts (p. 13).

A good social studies lesson has an oral discussion component. Literature with social studies concepts encourages a thinking citizen by teaching the process of defending, explaining and expressing thoughts (p. 13).

When historical fiction is integrated with current events, science, art, music, writing, poetry and architecture and made a total experience, children learn to make connections (p. 13).

It is the making of these connections that turns a student into a thinking, responsive and caring citizen, which is after all the main purpose of social studies and all education (pp. 13–14).

Literature can express adequately that communities differ, that people develop rules to protect themselves depending on cultural values and environmental factors, that holidays reflect values, and that geographic factors affect living conditions (p. 14).

Source: Farina, C. (1989). *Making Connections: A K–12 Multicultural Literature Bibliography*. New York: New York City Board of Education. (Address: 110 Livingston Street, Brooklyn, NY 11201).

---

parents, community members, and faculty members to show the rationale for making curricular connections.

Farina (1989) discusses ten key concepts that are important in multicultural education:

1. Change
2. Citizenship
3. Culture
4. Empathy
5. Environment
6. Identity
7. Interdependence
8. Nation/State
9. Scarcity
10. Technology

The two "Core Curriculum" teaching modules show how to use these concepts to make curricular connections. (See Section III, Teaching Modules 1 and 2.) For example, in making connections with science and geography, the first instruction in each module asks students to list site-specific weather, vegetation, climate, and sensory data they find in the book they are reading, and to name the character who supplies the data. Then students are asked to draw what they have described. This activity links the key concepts of environment, identity, and empathy (and enables students to use multiple intelligences, as well as critical-thinking skills). In another activity, "Gap Generation," students have a chance to ask questions about details of family life depicted in the work being studied—and how these customs relate to the key concepts.

Other activities involve letter writing, mapping, and mathematics problem solving—all based on the work of literature being read. Worksheets are provided for students to use for character development ("Bubble Your Way to Character Study") and making predictions about plots ("Beginnings and Endings").

Strategy 14. First Ladies in Profile (F.L.I.P.)—Trading Cards Research Project

Using Technology to Explore the F.L.I.P. Side of the Presidency (Grades 4–8)

Although television, newspapers, and films have helped make the U.S. First Ladies recognizable, few students can name, much less discuss, any First Ladies beyond the current one or immediate-past-Presidents' wives, such as Nancy Reagan and Barbara Bush. On the other hand, the names and lives of baseball players who were active in the 1950s and '60s are quite vivid to the preteen baseball card enthusiasts in my classes. As I watched them trading cards before class, I decided that we might use technology with the trading-cards concept as a tool for involving the students in First Lady studies.

Getting Started

I surprised the students by asking them to bring in their trading cards of all kinds for critical review and possible replication in our computer lab, using drawing and word processing software. At the supermarket, I stocked up on some baseball, football, hockey, and *Star Trek* cards.

The next day I distributed my newly acquired collection throughout the class and divided my students into trade-collection teams (of three or four students each). I gave the teams 10 minutes to come up with the format and packaging guidelines for their batch of mixed (baseball, football, hockey, *Star Trek*) trading cards. They worked at two computer monitors, one of which had word processing software booted up while the other had drawing software. (Note: More time can be allotted for this design analysis, if necessary.)

After the students had a chance to develop group format and packaging guidelines, I asked each team to read the guidelines they came up with for their batch of cards from their monitors.

As each team presented their ideas, I listed those common to all types of trading cards on a large projection screen (you could also use a large monitor).

My students initially identified the following guidelines:

Color Picture/Photo Backing/Portrait
Vital Statistics: Age, height, weight
Geographic Statistics: Team, league
Sport Achievements: Averages, key plays, prizes, records set
Brief Introductions . . . Quotes from or about players
Player's nicknames
Wrapping paper with name of trading card—10 cards per wrapper

After the students had developed these generic trading card guidelines, I told them that each team was about to use the drawing software to start their own trading card company. I explained that they would work on an often neglected group of famous women—our First Ladies.

I assigned each team about eight First Ladies to research. [Note: If *Compton's Online Encyclopedia* or presidential-themed software packages (including databases and timelines) are available, these resources can be used.] The teams had three in-class periods for the project—two for research and the third to put together their trading card designs.

Branching Out

Communication Arts/Advertising/Marketing. The name "F.L.I.P." came from the marketing pitch developed by one of the teams. They called them FLIP cards (originally for the drawing program's FLIP command but then modified to meet our "First Ladies in Profile" research theme). The packaged cards bore the motto, "Have you read to your child today?—Help our libraries!" and the wrapping paper was designed in our computer lab. The cards focused on various First Ladies' causes. The cards were sold in our neighborhood and school libraries, with the proceeds going for books.

Each team developed a marketing plan and an advertising campaign for their cards. They put this campaign together as a 30-second slide show. They kept track of sales, and they made videotapes. Several students developed board games to go with their trading cards.

Research/Improvisation/Role Play: In the process of developing their trading cards, one team used the cards for a "First Ladies Quantum Leap Lunch." They had members of their improvisation troupe pick cards at random and prepare to role-play what the First Ladies would say at lunch. Once the role-players had finished their review of their trading "background" card, they sat down to a fictional lunch where they talked about their husbands and their lives.

Creative Writing/Romances. One of my students was struck by the romance angle of several of the First Ladies' stories. He and a friend collaborated on writing the romance of Andrew and Rachel Jackson. Another student read about cases Mary Lincoln got involved in after Abe Lincoln's death. That student wrote a diary detailing Mary's thoughts during her crisis. The students published a *First Ladies' Private Lives* series of booklets written in the Harlequin Romance style.

Social Concerns/Community Outreach: Telecommunications. Some of my students had met Barbara Bush during one of her library visits on behalf of literacy. They were impressed by her mission to improve social literacy. As we anticipated the '92 Presidential Campaign, some of the students canvassed our community and their school friends through our computer bulletin board to survey appropriate '92 First Ladies' Social Action causes.

They developed a list of five Social Action causes—drug abuse, incest, vandalism, racism, and dropouts—they felt the new First Lady (or Barbara Bush) should advocate. They wrote letters to the White House and the candidates' wives promoting their selections. These projects reinforced students' skills in both letter writing and persuasive writing—and enhanced their awareness of societal issues.

In this activity, the use of technology greatly speeded our surveys and the responses.

Through all the "F.L.I.P." activities, access to technology enhanced the graphic arts quality of our cards, allowed us to publish greater quantities of cards, and standardized the format of our *First Ladies' Private Lives* series. Technology also assisted in the assessment of student work through the maintenance of electronic student portfolios and the easy production of cards, marketing materials, and books.

As we continue our "F.L.I.P." trading cards project, I look forward to further curricular activities that evolve from our computer-supported "cards on the table."

Strategy 15.
Newspapers in Education

In a world where the daily newspaper includes stories of alien smugglers, small children being thrust into traffic by their parents, concealed asbestos threats in public schools, communities destroyed by floods, and deliberate terrorist attacks, I feel that the role of the classroom teacher is not only to instruct students in basic skills, but also to engage students in examining, evaluating, and participating in the community. The newspapers provide the classroom teacher with a living text of actual critical-thinking issues that not only develop reading, writing, oral communication, and problem-solving skills, but also offer students an opportunity to evolve their own citizenship roles, including multicultural understandings. By using technology as an electronic notepad and recorder of group discussions, students can engage in proactive citizenship activities as part of their daily routine. Technology has also assisted in the evaluation of student work and peer assessments of products and projects. The activities that evolved into the "Newspapers in Education" strategy show var-

ied ways to infuse the study of newspapers across the curriculum and encourage the discovery process for students, parents, and community members. Some of the activities are definitely tied to current affairs and can be easily modified to fit the circumstances of any community or current issues.

Strategy 15a. "Responsibility" and "Values" in the News

Admire/Bother. In line with my social action goals (Banks 1991), I used a time period when my students regularly studied newspapers in class. I asked my 6th grade students—an ethnically diverse class—to form teams of two to three students each. I asked all team members to cut out from the newspaper, events, trends, people, or movements they either "admired" or were "bothered" by. One student from each team was to be designated as the clipping coordinator. Another student was asked to record (in a computer file) which specific events, trends, people, or movements were admired or that bothered the team members. The student teams were given 15 to 20 minutes for this independent news reading. (See Module 3a in the "Responsibilities and Values" Teaching Module in Section III.)

Interestingly, with this "admire"/"bother" news focus, the teams who could usually wrap up independent reading asked for more time to get their responses together. Recorders who were keeping track of the news items that students admired and that bothered them said they needed time to enter all the comments. After the student teams had had sufficient time to develop their own clippings and lists, they shared their responses with the whole class.

As each individual team clipper and recorder presented the team's views, I encouraged group discussion. The initial "recorder" team files were printed out to add to the discussion. However, I purposely refrained from comment. This was my students' chance to articulate their views as citizens.

Among the items that bothered my 6th graders were the smuggling of illegal aliens, the death of forty people in a Turkish hotel as a result of a fire set by terrorists, the prolonged custody battle over a two-year-old girl originally given up for adoption by her biological mother, the use of steroids by athletes, the asbestos threat in a city elementary school, the way the Cuban government had foiled some citizens' escapes, and the tragedy caused in Mississippi by rising floodwaters.

The student discussion dwelt not so much on arguing about which items should be included, but on articulating what was "sad" or "wrong" about them.

Among the few items that students "admired" were the selection of Tansu Cillen as the first woman Prime Minister of Turkey, Jean Bertrand Aristide, Nelson Mandela, and the work of the Habitat for Humanity.

Without instructor prompting, the students shared some of their ideas for changing the situations, laws, and community actions that seemed to be responsible for the things that bothered them. The following are some of their spontaneous responses to the previously identified issues:

- There should be laws that prevent even biological mothers from getting back their children (whom they have agreed to put up for adoption) after a year.
- The government should assist smuggled aliens, not deport them.
- Parents, children, and teachers need to be better informed about asbestos threats and more active in working to close schools where such threats are found to be real.
- Students should be allowed to assist in the Habitat for Humanity efforts.
- Clothes, canned food, and appliances should be collected by students to be sent to Mississippi flood victims.

Social Action Focus. Banks' (1991) theories of multicultural education include the social action approach as the desired highest level of multicultural studies. As part of the social action approach, students and teachers are asked to devise ways of "doing real things," based on their learning, that change or network with the adult civic community. The students' spontaneous initiatives outlining social and legislative change were very much in line with these theories.

To further focus my young students on citizenship and social action concerns, I asked them to spend another independent newspaper-reading period circling, recording (in computer files), or clipping words from the newspaper that they felt were "Responsibility" or "Values" words. I purposely did not have any prediscussion with the students because I wanted them to decide on their own, in their groups, which words fit these topics. I asked that the recorders not only enter the words found, but also keep notes on the groups' discussions.

The student groups took 20 minutes for their word searches. As I circulated among the groups without commenting, I heard comments such as: "Is 'rebuke' a 'values' word? . . . Sure, it means someone doesn't approve! . . . 'Deplore'— what does that mean? It certainly sounds bad. . . . 'Censure' is a definite for responsibilities and action."

Again, after the students had finished identifying the words, they shared the words they had found through their individual team searches. The lists of words were printed out so everyone could examine them.

Among the "values" words in the news identified by the students were: censures, deplores, scold, blamed, assail, needy, stymied, and condemns.

The students decided that some of these same words also were "responsibility" words:

If you "blame" someone or a group, it means you're saying he, she, or it is "responsible" for what he/she/it has done.

"Assail" is a strong "responsibility" word. . . . A group gangs up on a country and really says it's their fault. To me that's "responsibility" with a capital "R".

Once the students had concluded their "values" and "responsibility" discussion, I asked them what they felt or had learned about the newspaper, if anything, from these two group exercises.

At first, the students were hesitant to respond. Finally, several students joined in the following discussion:

> I never read the news for responsibility. I always felt the newspaper just recorded what happened without giving "value" opinions, but now I see the words used do give "value" ideas. But now as I look at the printouts, I see how many words our teams and the other teams came up with.

> And I never really looked into headlines to see all the "words" that broadcast those newspaper reporters' views on responsibility. You know what? I don't agree with some of the values used by the reporters.

> I never asked myself if I "admired" or was "bothered" by anything I read in the newspaper.

> Me, too. I didn't think I had any part in judging what happened in the newspaper or the way it was written.

> I think this was a waste of time. We're kids, who cares what we think, anyhow?

> No, we made up a list of stuff we could do. I want to call up that Habitat group and see if we can get them to come to work in my neighborhood.

> And we can do a canned food, game, and clothing drive for the families from our school.

The teams and I then compiled a list of student concerns. (For an example, see Module 3b in the "Responsibilities and Values" Teaching Module in Section III. These "Cases to Consider," of course, reflected what we were reading about at the time. Other teachers and students would, naturally, compile their own list.) As a next step, students completed Module 3c, "Social Action Reactions," which helped in bringing the news to a personal level.

Bills of Responsibility. Because the majority of the students were excited by their part in this project, I decided to extend that activism by having them draw on their news findings to author their own "Bills of Responsibility." In 1985 a group of businesspeople, political leaders, community activists, and teachers had gathered together at Valley Forge to author a Bill of Responsibilities. (See Module 3d in the "Responsibilities and Values" Teaching Module in Section III.) The Bill was modeled on the Declaration of Independence and Bill of Rights formats. It included a Preamble followed by a listing of the responsibilities, articulated as "To _____" statements.

I told the students that they would now have the same opportunity the Valley Forge group had—the chance to author their own "Bill of Responsibility." I handed out copies of the "Valley Forge" Bill of Responsibility and blank worksheets (see Modules 3d and 3e in the "Responsibilities and Values" Teaching Module) to the teams and encouraged them to use their "Responsibilities" and "Values" clippings file, lists, and discussion notes to develop their Bills. Among the resource materials I had collected for my Responsibility unit was a pictorial, ten-panel representation of the Bill of Rights. To provide a spatial entry point (Gardner 1991) for my visual learners and some of the students who had less than two years of English-language schooling experience, I referred to this illustration and suggested that teams could either "draw" (using our *MacDraw* computer graphics program) or write or provide dual written and pictorial Bills of Responsibility. Then I gave the teams a full class period for their drafts.

When I circulated among the drafters, I noted that the Preamble seemed to be a stumbling block, so I made a "public" announcement that the teams could leave the Preamble for the end of the process or omit it if it were too difficult. Many of the teams then began work on their "Bills of Responsibilities." I noticed that, with two exceptions, each of the teams developed a "drawn" Bill. We then completed and printed out these Bills and pictorial representations.

The "drafters" each stood in front of the class to read and display their "Bills of Responsibilities." The Bills included many news-based concerns:

- To give everyone a chance for jobs
- To provide safe, clean homes for the poor
- To rescue and accept Haitian and Chinese immigrants
- To protect the rights of young children whose parents abuse them or are unable to protect them
- To provide aid for victims of floods
- To make certain schools and apartments are asbestos free
- To provide medical services to poor families
- To make certain that citizens are protected against terrorists

The displayed printouts were posted on a special "Bill of Responsibility" wall and revised as news and community events warranted. These changing printouts and exhibits—as well as the community feedback we received— formed an essential part of the ongoing assessment of the "Bills and Responsibilities" project.

Students also shared their Bills (both written and drawn) with their families. One parent added some Responsibilities in Spanish. Another student's older brother provided his own graphic additions to our pictorial Bills. The students then began co-drafting a "Bill of Responsibility" with the Wedgwood senior citizen group—one of their members was a grandparent who served as our liaison for the group.

Through continued classroom monitoring and recording of the news, team meetings, and social-action initiatives derived from student reactions, middle school students can begin to play responsible, active, citizenship roles in their community. Not only can they articulate values and responsibilities, but also they can start assuming them.

Strategy 15b. Cultural Collages: Multicultural Awareness Newspaper Investigation

As a lifelong newspaper reader, I have always noticed how a particular theme, story, or issue will often pervade both printed and broadcast news coverage. This media blitz can last a week—or span a month or two. My middle school students and I have tracked a particular theme, such as "Children as Victims of Random Violence" or "School Personnel Using Drugs," by doing collages that mixed themed headlines and graphics (photos/graphics/ads) as they appeared in a variety of dailies over a given time period. These dated "Cultural Collages" have formed a visual arts research product that helped us integrate current events and critical newspaper reading into our study of social issues.

After several recent racial incidents in the community, I decided to enter into a very touchy and uncomfortable classroom terrain by examining newspaper coverage of racial and cultural groups. To what extent did this coverage celebrate and support the intricate mosaic? We decided to call this project the "Multicultural Awareness Newspaper Investigation."

Getting Started. I listed the following racial/ethnic groups on the blackboard: Blacks, Hispanics, Chinese, Japanese, Koreans, Jews, Indians, Native Americans, Haitians, Dominican Republicans, Puerto Ricans, Greeks, and Irish.

I asked the students to work together in "Eyewitness News Reader" teams to predict how many news items (including stories or graphics) and what news sections these ethnic/racial groups would appear in. The groups were given 3–5 minutes to confer together and come up with their predictions.

I then asked each team to share their predictions, as well as the rationale behind the group's final consensus. A recorder listed the predictions for each ethnic group on the board next to each group.

After the groups had shared their predictions, I gave each group two different daily newspapers, as well as two manila file folders, scissors, and a glue stick. I told the students that they would have a chance to check and confirm their own predictions by going through the newspapers given their team. Then I distributed a "Cultural Collage Multicultural Awareness News Investigation" worksheet (see Section III, Worksheet 11).

The students and I reviewed the sheet together. I suggested that each team select one student to record the number of times and in which news sections various ethnic/racial groups were mentioned. In addition, I asked that one student collect the headlines, photos, or graphics that featured these groups. Finally, one group member was asked to "collage" the headlines, photos, and graphics onto opened manila folders (for instructions for making "Pop-Up Manila Folders," see Section III, Worksheet 12). I provided markers if these cultural "currents" artists wanted to embellish their collages further. The students had 20–25 minutes to complete their investigations and make their collages.

After the students independently reviewed their newspapers, each group was given an opportunity to share their reactions to the actual number of multicultural references in the news. Each group analyzed the accuracy of their predictions and some of the news factors that affected the predictions.

Next, I had the students focus on the list of ethnic and racial groups we had initially explored. I asked each team to review their findings and examine their collages to decide

whether the references found were positive, negative, or neutral and to what extent they presented a valid or stereotyped image of the ethnic or racial group. The students were also allowed to make an initial determination of insufficient evidence if they felt they didn't have enough citations to make a judgment in any category. A group discussion period of 5 minutes was allotted for this analysis.

After each team had discussed the nature and validity of multicultural images projected in the news, we opened the discussion up to involve all teams. First, I asked each team to hold up and display their collages. Then I requested that whoever spoke for the team be sure to refer to the specific collages as the team's or individuals' evaluations were presented.

As various class members presented their views, I listed them on the board without comment. The students debated one another's judgments by making reference to the news.

Among the consensus findings of our first "Multicultural Awareness Newspaper Investigation" were:

• The images and citations of blacks in the news that day were mostly negative.

• Many visual/verbal associations with black people dealt with crime, low academic scores, and poverty. The only positive article dealt with an athlete.

• There were few references to Hispanics, Indians, Greeks, or Native Americans that day. Therefore, there were insufficient data to make a judgment of media coverage.

• Puerto Ricans were favorably featured in one article, but there were still insufficient data to make a judgment.

• The Chinese were most favorably covered, with an emphasis on academic success and artistic ability. Many students, some of whom were Chinese, worried about the news perpetuating a too-favorable, unrealistic stereotype. Was this just as bad as a denigrating stereotype? The students were divided on this question.

• The same issue came up with the image of Japanese economic success.

• Was every reference to "Israel" a reference to Jews? Several students volunteered to research that one.

• The only story on Dominican Republicans in New York City was part of a series on sons of immigrants who played on an after-school baseball team. One of my students said he had read several stories of successful but poor Dominican Republican students on baseball teams. None of the other students could ever recall a story on this group which didn't deal with baseball. Was that a desirable stereotype, or could baseball expertise possibly be the only newsworthy aspect of the Dominican Republican New York experience?

Branching Out. Students opted to do an in-depth Multicultural News Awareness study of specific groups. They spent two weeks collecting references, preparing collages, and evaluating their findings. These were shared in a Multicultural News Awareness Forum, with reporter participants and community members.

Several students collected only news photos and graphic depictions of one group. They called their photographic survey "Multicultural Images in the News." These students found that through its selection of images, the news perpetuated, created, or defused stereotypes. These student-developed surveys formed an important part of the peer-review process of assessment.

As a result of our initial research, two students set up a database of multicultural stories and references.

Another project involved an investigation of Fourteenth Amendment "Equal Protection" aspects of our initial researches. Students took various cases to our local chapter of the American Civil Liberties Union to explore what the legal aspects of this coverage might be.

Although many uncomfortable, provocative, and tense remarks surfaced during our study, our breakthrough discussion of these social issues was somewhat distanced and defused by

their news base. Through "Cultural Collages," we began to formulate a news perspective on the state of our dynamic cultural mosaic. Such student-centered investigations and studies initiate students, teachers, and the community into necessary multicultural social dialogue. Through community feedback and oral discussions, as well as the evaluation of our changing collages, we were able to enjoy an ongoing assessment of our work.

Strategy 15c. Hero Rites

As the 25th anniversary of the assassination of Bobby Kennedy approached, I began writing a tribute to him in my own journal. I wanted to share my feelings about this personal hero with my 6th graders. Yet I hesitated. For me, Bobby had been a strong visual and oral presence during my teen years. To my students, who were born in the 1980s, he was at best a name from the past or a fuzzy videotape image of a thin white man in an oversized jacket. How could I link up my multiethnic, '90s students with a '60s hero who died before they were born? Should I share my emotions at all?

I decided to use my own reflections and sentiments about a personal hero to engage my students in exploring their own concepts of heroism.

Getting Started. I began by asking the students to work together in groups to list those individuals they felt were heroes today (see "Hero Rites" in Section III, Worksheet 13). The students were given 5 minutes to come up with their lists in groups. Then they shared their lists of heroes as a class. Among the contemporary heroes identified by the students were Magic Johnson, Michael Jordan, Michael Jackson, Arthur Ashe, Ryan White, Arnold Schwarzenegger, Macauley Culkin, their own mothers, firefighters, some teachers, Patrick Ewing, Bobby Bonilla, Bart Simpson, and Sharon Stone. Martin Luther King, George Washington, and Abraham Lincoln appeared on only four of thirty-one lists developed. Those heroes whose names appeared on almost all the lists were Magic Johnson and Michael Jordan.

As I listened to my students talk about their heroes, what struck me was the absence of political leaders, educators, writers, judges, lawyers, civic advocates, and women (other than some individual votes for their mothers and a few female teachers). In the '60s, a list of student heroes would have been filled with political figures. Also, I found it interesting that five out of my eleven student teams included Bart Simpson, an animated, anti-establishment comic character on *The Simpsons*, as a hero. Not only was their choice of this particular animated character interesting—but the fact that he was included on a list of *human* heroes.

I decided to use Bart as a jumping-off figure. I put the following questions on the board: Why did many of you include a cartoon character? What is a hero to you? How would you define the word *hero* today? Can or should cartoon, animation, and/or literary characters be included as heroes?

I decided to have the students examine their own concepts of hero individually. Therefore, I told them to take 10 minutes or more, as needed, to answer either one or all of the questions. I suggested they might also use the time to just write down their thoughts on what it is to be a hero (see Worksheet 13, "Hero Rites").

During the 10 minutes, some of my 6th graders sat in uncharacteristic silence, contemplating the questions. Toward the end of the time span, when I cautioned the students that only 3 minutes were left, these reflective 6th graders started writing. Other students wrote throughout the time. Some wrote and then crossed out or "whited out" ideas.

The students were then given a chance to share their individual definitions of heroes, give their responses to the questions, or just voice their views on heroes. I listened as they shared their ideas:

A hero is strong and brave.
A hero does admirable things.
To be a hero is to help others.
A hero is someone who saves a life.
A hero is someone who is admired
by others.

If you risk your own life for others you may be a hero. If you die doing it, you are definitely a hero. My uncle died in Vietnam—he was a hero.

Some jobs are "hero jobs." Firemen, police, and hospital workers are heroes. Their jobs are to help and rescue others.

My dad is my hero. I try to be like him.

People who care about others are heroes. The students in our class are heroes because they are sponsors of a child. [Our 6th grade class had sponsored an African child through the Save the Children campaign.]

Bart is a hero because he stands up for what he believes in. A hero has to be a real person to count. Heroes do real-life things.

As the students spoke, one student recorded their definitions. I suggested that we extend our "Hero Rites" beyond the classroom. I asked each student to interview three individuals, including at least two adults of different ages. The students could either start with their own definitions or ask their interview subjects to give their definitions of heroes. The students were also encouraged to share their own lists of heroes. They were given a week for this "Heroic Outreach" oral history survey.

The results of the survey were eye openers for the students and for me. Indeed, they motivated the students to do further research into historical, political, audio, and film heroes. Among the heroes suggested by the adults surveyed were such "unfamiliar" or "vaguely recognizable" (to 11-year-old multiethnic students) names as: Mahatma Gandhi, General deGaulle,

Mother Hale, Eleanor Roosevelt, Dwight Eisenhower, Justice William Douglas, Willie Mays, Rosa Parks, Sandy Koufax, the Green Hornet, John F. Kennedy, Franklin Roosevelt, Bob Dylan, the Beatles, and John Wayne. Other more familiar but not really "known about" heroes suggested by the adults included: Nelson Mandela, Gloria Steinem, Toni Morrison, Alice Walker, Thurgood Marshall, Norman Siegel, Ralph Nader, Lech Walesa, Pope John Paul II, Cardinal O'Connor, and Herman Badillo.

Branching Out. As the students shared the heroes identified by their adult subjects, they would often end their reports with a statement like this: "I have to look her up. . . . I want to learn more about her." One outcome of this "Heroic Outreach" project was individual student research into unfamiliar heroes. Another unexpected benefit of the student interviews was an increase in unassigned student newspaper reading and newsbroadcast viewing.

"That guy Badillo who's running for Comptroller is the same Herman Badillo on my list?" asked one student. When I told him that was the same "hero," the student started clipping out articles to follow the hero's current activities.

One parent was pleasantly surprised when her daughter asked her to record an interview Gloria Steinem was going to give on a late night show. "I want to hear what she has to say to see if I think she's a hero," said the young woman of 11 who had learned of Ms. Steinem's existence through interviewing her mother's best friend. The same young lady felt really excited about the "Take Our Daughters to Work" day launched by the Ms. Foundation because it produced a flow of interviews with and articles about Gloria Steinem.

Once the students were somewhat grounded in secondary, primary, and media source material explicating the lives of the heroes from their "Heroic Outreach" list, they were given an opportunity to decide whether they agreed or disagreed with these individuals'

being designated as heroes. Each student was asked to make an oral presentation defending or opposing the individual's "hero" status. After each presentation, the student presenter led a discussion of whether or not the class members felt the individual profiled was really a hero.

During one of these presentations, one student noted that of the six people he had interviewed about John F. Kennedy, three felt he had been a hero, but two said they had lost respect for him since his death. "So someone can be considered a hero twenty years ago but may not be considered one today," observed the student. Another student suggested that some individual heroes like Lech Walesa, Mikhail Gorbachev, and Nelson Mandela could be heroes to the world but be looked down on in their own countries.

Finally, I asked the students to review their original group lists of heroes and personal definitions. They were given time to modify their original parameters of *hero*. Some of the lists were greatly expanded. Most lists had at least one or two new names on them and had lost several names. Among the added qualities of heroes included in the definition revisions were:

> A hero speaks out for what he believes in even though others don't like him.

> To be a hero is to fight for social justice and equal treatment for all, including women.

> A hero can write or lead protests to make people aware of changes needed.

Perhaps the best indication of the impact of our "Hero Rites" on the students' growth as thinkers, citizens, and writers was one definition many students agreed with:

> The definition of hero can change from year to year for many people or even for one person. But it is still important to study and to talk about heroes. We all need heroes to give us people we can be like in our lives.

The ongoing "Hero Rites" project had provided my evolving citizens with a focus for continuing examination of their own and the community's ideals.

Strategy 15d. Mayoral Family Find

This "Newspapers in Education" project evolved as a way to extend newspaper reading (and writing about news items) to involve family members in learning activities. The project, which uses a modification of the "Family Find" worksheet (see Section III, Worksheet 14), centered around the local mayoral campaign and the media blitz it occasioned.

"Mayoral Family Find," like the other newsreader activities, involved students in a creative, analytical discovery process. Its purposes were:

• To involve students and families in targeted news, family learning activities

• To provide students with an introduction to format journals

• To engage students, teachers, and families in ongoing discussion and analysis of the mayoral campaign

At the beginning of the mayoral campaign, I invited parents and other family members of my students to come to class to participate in a *New York Newsday* "Newspapers in Education" workshop. I asked family members to work together as a team to find news articles, photos, and graphics that interested them and to put together the first page of a scrapbook they would keep for several weeks. At the end of the class period, I asked the students and their families to work together at home to keep journals and clippings in their scrapbooks, focusing on the current political campaign for the mayor's office. (See Teaching Modules 4a and 4b, "News-paper Discovery: Family Learning Scrapbook and Journal.")

As the project continued, the students and I kept track of progress and planned culminating activities to celebrate our success and share our findings. (See Section III, "Mayoral Family F.I.N.D." Teaching Module, for a complete description of this activity, along with modified "Mayoral Family F.I.N.D." worksheets.)

Though many of our language arts and social studies projects have involved a substantial visual product, other multicultural projects have been arts driven, as described in the next chapter.

❧   ❧   ❧

References

Baker, G.C. (1994). *Planning and Organizing for Multicultural Instruction*. 2nd ed. Menlo Park, Calif.: Addison-Wesley.

Banks, J.A. (1991). *Teaching Strategies for Ethnic Studies*. 5th ed. Boston: Allyn and Bacon.

Farina, C. (1989). *Making Connections: A K–12 Multicultural Literature Bibliography*. New York: New York City Board of Education. (Address: 110 Livingston Street, Brooklyn, NY 11201).

Gardner, H. (1983). *Frames of Mind*. New York: Basic Books.

Gardner, H. (1991). *The Unschooled Mind*. New York: Basic Books.

Gardner, H. (1993). *Multiple Intelligences*. New York: Basic Books.

Machachlan, P. (1985). *Sarah, Plain and Tall*. New York: Harper.

Mohr, N. (1979). *Felita*. New York: Barton, Skylark.

Olivanes, R.A. (1993). *Using the Newspaper to Teach ESL Learners*. Newark, Del.: International Reading Association.

5 Multidisciplinary Multicultural Arts

Through the creation of an object of art, much learning about the self and others can take place.

> Gwendolyn Baker,
> *Planning and Organizing*
> *for Multicultural Instruction*
> (1994, p. 158)

If we put images of minorities in the classroom, even if we say nothing about them, they can help kids develop more positive attitudes.

> James A. Banks, *Teaching Tolerance*
> (1992, p. 23)

In America's communities and classrooms, where children of several ethnic backgrounds often live and work together . . . arts can be a language of understanding.

> Jo Miles Schuman,
> *Art from Many Hands* (1980)

Teacher to Teacher

I can see how arts projects are a natural for an art teacher who wants to integrate ethnic content and multicultural awareness across the curriculum, but why should I as a teacher of language arts or social studies venture into arts-driven projects? My mission is to engage my students, their parents, our school, and our neighborhood community in multicultural studies. Why should I—with no special talents in arts and no training in arts instruction—use arts projects? Aren't all the writing, reading, broadcasting, performance, interview, and newspaper projects sufficient? Some of them have arts as-

pects, like storyboarding multicultural literature. Isn't that enough in the arts area?

These activities are *not* enough, if many of the students you're trying to engage learn in a style that mainly uses their spatial capacities or if they have not yet become sufficiently fluent in spoken English to fully demonstrate their linguistic capacities.

Benefits of Multicultural Arts Projects

Many students can immediately share ethnic content through a spatial-learner-friendly format, such as a "Cultural Greeting Card," that immediately empowers them to share cultural information. Kinesthetic, auditory (musical-oral), spatial, intrapersonal, and interpersonal capacities can be engaged by serving, discussing, sharing, and critiquing fortune cookies (as in the "Fortune Cookies" strategy). Finally, by engaging almost all intelligence capacities—auditory (musical), interpersonal, intrapersonal, spatial, linguistic, and kinesthetic—students can literally compile, illustrate, handbind, and share favorite literature with family members (as in the "Gifts of Literacy" strategy).

Multidisciplinary, multicultural arts outcomes are important for providing a spatial entry point to multicultural education. Engaging students in the arts broadens access to multicultural understanding, not only for all students but also for parents and community members (Gardner 1983, 1991, 1993). And infusing multicultural perspectives into the arts enhances both content and skills acquisition for students and promotes lifelong learning.

Strategy 16.
Cultural Greeting Cards

A Multidisciplinary Research Project

Despite stated multicultural goals, the approach of the winter and spring holidays finds ethnically diverse elementary and middle students involved in celebrations of the Judeo-Christian holidays and traditional American customs. Though some professionals would argue that students' participation in seasonal chorales, pageants, plays, and activities draws them into the American community, it also effectively prevents them from sharing their own cultural/ethnic celebrations. Not only does this lack of opportunity to share their ethnic roots work against nurturing culturally diverse students' unique identities, but it also deprives the school community as a whole of pluralistic seasonal holiday perspectives. Such perspectives would not only enhance the students' school experience, but promote *intergroup respect* that will lay the foundation for proactive citizenship in a pluralistic society. To engage ethnically diverse students in seasonal celebrations, my students and I have evolved our "Cultural Greeting Cards" project.

Getting Started

First, I collected greeting cards in different languages, including Italian, Spanish, Chinese, Korean, Haitian Creole, and Japanese, from card stores in various ethnically diverse neighborhoods in New York City. I brought them into my 5th grade class and asked those students who understood the words on them to help

translate them for the rest of us. Several students proudly got up to explain the messages on the cards.

Interestingly, other students said that although they were from a particular language background represented on the card, they couldn't read the language. Several of my ten-year-olds observed that they used to speak or read their native language but were in the process of forgetting how to. Two students asked if they could take the cards home to get them translated. I responded by asking them to bring in their relatives with the translations. We set a date when family members who spoke languages other than English could come in to our classroom.

In preparation for the visit, I asked the students to generate questions for their guests about seasonal celebrations and holiday greetings in their native countries. Our guests shared not only their translations of the original foreign-language greeting cards we had collected but also their cultural holiday and seasonal traditions. Among those holidays and traditions discussed were: Kwanza, the winter solstice, the corn ritual, Chanukah, and Lunar New Year.

The students asked about the kinds of gifts given and the songs or rituals that accompany that particular ethnic celebration. For example, they learned that on each of the seven days of Kwanza, a candle is lit in a Kinara (candleholder), a principle of black culture is discussed, and some gifts (including homemade ones) are exchanged.

One of our Chinese parents, Grace's dad, Mr. Lee, explained (in Chinese—Grace translated) that Lunar New Year is a several-weeks-long holiday season with New Year's Day falling in the middle. Cards, lucky money envelopes, and papers for writing lucky sayings are all in red, the special Chinese color for good luck. Traditional lucky couplets are written on red paper and pasted on doorposts. Red envelopes of lucky money are given to children and unmarried relatives.

This section is adapted from "Cultural Greeting Cards," *Notes Plus*, December 1993. Copyright © 1993 by the National Council of Teachers of English. Adapted by permission.

Justin pointed out that Jewish children get Chanukah "gelt" or money, as well.

At the end of our discussion, I invited the students to design their own cultural greeting cards, which would include the knowledge about diverse ethnic celebrations they had learned from our guests. Maria and Justin asked one of our Chinese guests to help them with writing an appropriate greeting phrase in Chinese on their card. I was surprised to see that at least one-third of my class set about designing cards for cultural celebrations other than their own. Several adult translators found themselves roving around the classroom, assisting with native-language writing, phrases, and cultural art representations. I observed their children glancing at them with pride.

During our card-design session, one grandparent from Korea came over to me with her granddaughter Elaine. Elaine told me her grandmother wanted me to know how reluctant she had been to come to school because she couldn't speak English. Although she had really worried about speaking to our class, Elaine's grandmother had enjoyed meeting the children. They had made her feel important—"like a teacher." She hadn't felt that way since she had arrived in the United States eight years before.

Branching Out

We displayed the students' multilingual, multiethnic "Cultural Greeting Cards." In subsequent years, my elementary school classes built on the pilot project by using computer drawing and banner software (Broderbund *KIDSCUTS* and *Print Shop Deluxe*) to mass-produce seasonal cultural greeting cards. During holiday seasons, they ran their own "Cultural Card Boutique," where they sold cards to the school population and community. Proceeds from the sale have been donated to the UNICEF fund to assist children in need all over the world. In the works are plans to use

our cultural card designs on tee shirts and mugs.

In addition to their own primary sources (family, community) for cultural celebration designs and customs, our eager cultural greeting card designers have also researched unfamiliar cultures from secondary resources. They have gone on their own to view graphics and print collections in museums that would normally only interest high school art majors. They put together their own cultural card exhibit, which featured sketches of various cross-cultural celebration designs and student-authored explanations of the various celebrations researched. The students also decided to work on a desktop-published catalog of their exhibit, with scanned designs included.

On the middle school/junior high level, I sent students off to survey and critique the variety and types of cultural greeting cards they found in their neighborhood card stores. Students were asked to purchase cards that celebrated diverse cultures. Depending on the neighborhood, some students reported finding only traditional Christmas, Chanukah, Passover, and Easter cards; whereas others brought in samples of a variety of cultural celebration designs.

Cultural Greeting Card Critique Project

The 7th grade language arts students suggested another extension of the project. Two students, Grace and Lynda, who were of Chinese extraction, were offended by the humorous depiction of a Chinese New Year card, as well as the message inside. They said this commercialized greeting, produced by one of the leading national greeting card companies, exploited stereotypical views of Chinese people. Sparked by their comments, the 7th grade language arts students began a "Cultural Greeting Card Critique Project." As part of this project, we collected both serious and humorous cultural greeting cards. The cards were analyzed for: appropriateness/correctness of cultural celebration, message/theme, appropriate depiction and use of cultural designs, negative or positive use of cultural/ethnic stereotypes, and the degree of good-natured or mean-spirited humor in the cards.

The students initially wrote their critiques. They then shared them aloud. Because many of the analysis categories were quite subjective and judgments for any given cultural greeting card also varied, the classroom discussion was quite spirited. The subjects of the most heated exchanges were the "mixed blessing" cards, which featured Hanukkah and Christmas images side by side. Although the disagreements on the applicability of particular cultural greetings could not be absolutely resolved, it was interesting to listen to students engage in a critical discussion of specific cultural values. Based on the discussions, some self-identified artists collaborated with classroom cultural experts on the design of various cards that connected cultures.

As I continue to work with both elementary and middle/junior high students on the "Cultural Greeting Cards" project, I am astonished by the way the study of diverse cultural greeting cards can serve as an authentic catalyst for primary and secondary source research and investigation, forums, study of art history, museum-going, student-authored catalogues, cultural studies, exhibits, oral history, parent/child shared learning experiences, community outreach, proactive global citizenship, cultural/graphics critiques, discussions of cultural correctness, computer graphic arts, and entrepreneurial endeavors. In turn, these authentic learning experiences lead to ongoing, meaningful assessments that include peer review of portfolios, exhibits, and community feedback. (See the "Assessment" Chart in Figure 2.2.)

This project offers infinite opportunities for multiethnic, culturally diverse students to develop an appreciation of one another's cultural celebration traditions. Through these connec-

tions, the project achieves its most significant value as a tool for promoting *present* intergroup understanding and *future* proactive global citizenship.

Note: Sample student-designed greeting cards and critiques are available on request. (Figure 5.1 shows two student-created multicultural greeting cards.)

FIGURE 5.1
Sample Student-Created Cultural Greeting Cards

Chinese Cultural Card

Islamic Cultural Card

Strategy 17.
Fortune Cookie Critiques

Using Fortune Cookies for Language Arts Enchantment

To accommodate my schedule, which includes numerous after-school workshops, meetings, and conferences, my husband and I have gotten used to ordering Chinese food for dinner. At the end of our meal, we enjoy opening our fortune cookies and sharing our fortunes.

I began collecting both our uneaten fortune cookies and our shared fortune slips. These fortunes turned out to be filled with infinite language arts possibilities for my upper elementary school students.

Getting Started

First, I collected enough of the uneaten cookies to give one to every child in the class. All the fortune cookies were passed around. Each student pulled out one. They ate their cookies and copied down the fortune pulled out.

The students were given 15–20 minutes to write on at least one of the following (see "Fortune Cookie Critics" in Section III, Worksheet 16):

• The meaning of the fortune itself
• The applicability or appropriateness of the fortune to the student who got it
• The open-ended quality of the fortune— how this fortune could fit everyone in some way

After 20 minutes, the students were still writing. When it came time to share, they were really eager to get up and talk. Almost everyone in class wanted to reveal his fortune. Consequently, our fortune readings took two full periods. They were punctuated by "What was your fortune?" queries, as well as "You bet!" responses (accompanied by laughter) when students explained how particularly flattering fortunes were just right for them.

As the students shared their fortunes, I sat back to transcribe the animated discussion— which was so focused that they did not notice I was writing. I commented only now and then.

Ramon: It says here, "You will inherit a large sum of money." Well, I know just what to do with it. Seriously, the fortune has a printed happy face icon on it.

Teacher: This is the perfect content for a fortune designed to keep its owner smiling, eating, and buying more foods. You can't go wrong with a positive optimistic saying like this set in the unspecified future. Anyone who opens this fortune would be proud and eager to claim it as his or her own. A winning commercial fortune choice.

Theresa: My fortune also has that smiling face icon printed on it. It reminds me of those happy faces I used to get in kindergarten. It says, "You are surrounded by good friends." I see some of them smiling, so I guess this fortune's really meant for them. But on the serious side, what if your so-called good friends are really false friends? This saying certainly doesn't invite . . . what's that vocabulary word—intro—oh yes, "introspection." It lulls you into what could be a false sense of self-satisfaction. But I can see why it's a successful commercial fortune.

Chris: Mine is the most comforting and most appropriate for a class. I wonder if whoever writes these fortunes realized we'd be eating the cookies and talking about them in class. This fortune, happy face included, says, "You will pass a difficult test that will make you happier." I think that's great. Does that mean we don't have to study for the test? Or that passing it will guarantee our happiness? Why? Wouldn't it be funny if the author of this fortune were a moonlighting Language Arts teacher?

Alisha: Well, if so, I'd say that Language Arts teacher could be the same one who put the happy faces on Theresa's kindergarten work. My fortune says, "Happiness begins with facing life with a smile and a wink."

Chris: Does that work if you don't study for a difficult test? [Laughter]

Many laughs, asides, and cross-conversations later, I asked my fortune cookie critics how they felt about this "Break-in to composition and conversation" activity.

Elaine: It was really great!

Justin: I never thought of doing anything with food and writing. In fact, my older brother, who works for a Chinese restaurant, said he'd get us 100 free cookies. I thought maybe we'd break them up and see how many different ones we could find.

Danius: You know, we could use this as a great activity for our peer-teaching classes with the 3rd graders. They could write what each saying means. Then they could tell if they agree.

Tatiyana: We could also have them paste the sayings on sheets and draw storyboards of what they mean.

Danius: Or they could write a story that goes with the fortune.

Linda: For that matter, I was going to say we should put all the sayings together in an envelope and each pick out one or two. Then the challenge would be to write stories that incorporated the sayings in some way.

Tatiyana: I think that's a great idea, Linda—mind if Danius and I use it with our peer-teaching class?

Linda: That's fine, as long as we try it out here.

Ronald: Would you have any objection, Ms. Reissman, if we did a frequency tally of how many times various sayings oc-

cur? I bet we'd find plenty of repeats in Justin's 100 cookies.

Aeshia: You know, I think each of us could bring in a large number of fortune cookies. They're cheap, and I have a feeling my neighborhood Chinese restaurant would donate some.

Grace: I think I could get us a donation, as well.

Ronald: The more cookies, the greater the sampling. We'll prepare a research paper on "saying" frequency. OK, Ms. R.?

Grace: But, you know—I want to ask my grandmother, how authentic a part of Chinese culture fortune cookies are. I would be interested in knowing how Chinese these cookies are or how commercial.

Theresa: Don't laugh. But I'm still fascinated by that happy face stamp on our fortunes. I've never seen a fortune cookies with a happy face stamped on it before.

Andrew: We could compare and contrast kinds of fortune cookie brands. The ones you gave out were wrapped in cellophane, some are loose and yellower. Yours were whiter and larger.

Migdalia: Comparative Chinese cookies consumers reports. I think that'll be a great composition.

Grace: Let's get the bite on!

Tatiyana: You know, we can have the peer-teaching group fill out a flowchart on a web of ideas based on fortune cookies as the core crunch kernel. In fact, while we're talking, I've done one of our ideas for using fortune cookies.

[Figure 5.2 shows the web that Tatiyana made, summarizing the students' discussion.]

I marvelled at the ideas and plans the class generated to follow up on our initial fortune cookie "crack-up." We later used the computer to draw some of our animated fortune cookie

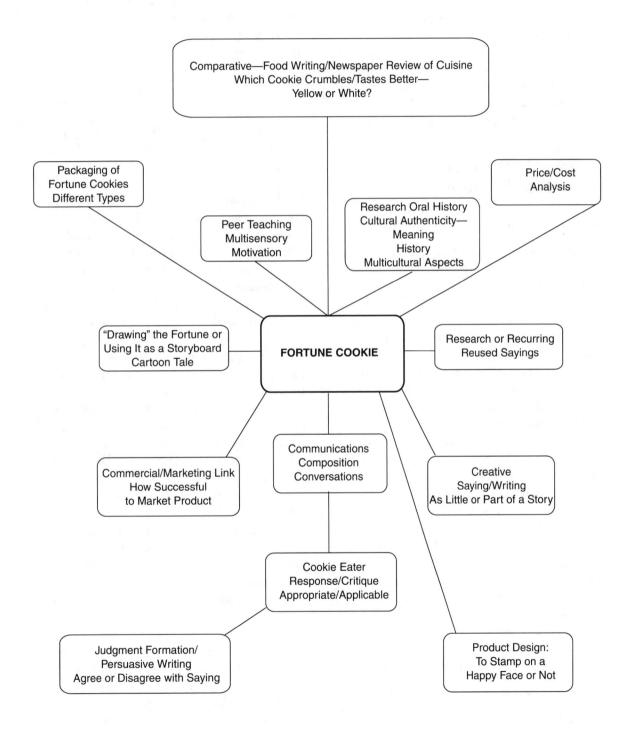

tales; create an initial, interactive, fortune-cookie animation piece where the students could fill in their own sayings; and hold on-line conversations about fortune cookies with students in other schools. We desktop-published much of our writing.

And peer teachers Danius and Tatiyana are still using the fortune cookies as an "opener" for their 3rd grade groups. Danius, Tatiyana, and the other students enjoy our "cookie core curriculum channel of consuming investigations."

Strategy 18.
Gift of Family Literacy

Student-Designed and -Produced Gift Books

On one of my regular browsing visits to the bookstore, I was struck by a series of small illustrated gift books, called *Belles Lettres* (1989). Although the series included literary works by Ralph Waldo Emerson, William Shakespeare, Mark Twain, Henry David Thoreau, Ambrose Bierce, Gertrude Stein, and Robert Louis Stevenson, the content wasn't what grabbed my attention. The series's initial drawing power was its undersized packaging design, complete with appropriate photographs, collage images, and graphics. The photos were hand-toned. The books had marbleized endsheets. Texts were a mix of two typefaces: Sabon and Clarendon. Because my students had already been involved with desktop publishing and knew something about what books are made of, *I knew I had to take these books to class.* I realized that the students had neither the funds nor the expertise to publish volumes exactly like these, but I intuitively felt that examining them could motivate the students to similar efforts—though on a more limited scale.

This section is adapted from "Give the Gift of Family Literacy—Student-Designed Gift Books," *English Journal*, October 1993. Copyright © 1993 by the National Council of Teachers of English. Adapted by permission.

I acted on my impulse and purchased several of these volumes for my own library. Then I also went through my home library to find other small-sized or oversized volumes of extraordinary design or beauty. My new project—involving an integrated Language Arts approach—had begun.

Getting Started

I decided to preorganize and presensitize my students to illustrated gift books and special design packages. I gave them three days to go through their own home libraries, the school library, and the public library (I could not in all good conscience ask them to browse through a bookstore and purchase an expensive book) for volumes in the fiction section that were of exceptional size, beauty, design, or format. As their assignment, I asked only that they bring in at least one volume that caught their attention and be prepared to show the volume and discuss its appeal.

On the day the assignment was due, I was most pleasantly surprised by the sea of beautiful books my students had collected. I wished I had brought in a camera to photograph the volumes they brought in. One was an old, brocade-bound book of Walt Whitman's poetry published in the early 1920s. The student whose aunt had lent it to her told me that she loved the feel of the poetry book and quoted her aunt as saying that just touching the book made her feel good. Another student brought in a family prayer book with a silver cover. To the student, this format showed that the prayers in the book were sacred, not for everyday use.

Although the students I initially piloted the project with were mature 5th and 6th graders, many of them brought in pop-up books. Two of these students said the books belonged to their younger siblings. But when I told the students I loved pop-up books myself and had purchased some for my niece and nephew, so I could enjoy them myself when I visited them, the whole class laughed. I also told the students that many adult theme books were done in pop-up format. They asked that I make a note for myself to bring in some of these adult pop-up books to share with them.

The students' independent selection of beautifully designed volumes was surprisingly rich and varied. Art and oversized coffee-table books I would never have thought of presenting to 10- and 11-year-olds were among the works students shared. I sat back in amazement as Migdalia shared an oversized volume of Chagall's art with a French text (Migdalia's family spoke Spanish). One student asked Migdalia why she selected a book written in a language she couldn't understand. Migdalia said she was fascinated by the paintings. They were magical in her mind. Other students had brought in large photography books on such nostalgic topics as movie stars of the silent screen and architecture.

On the other end of the size scale, students selected some of the Beatrix Potter *Peter Rabbit* books, books shaped like hearts, and some of the *See and Touch* books designed for young children. As the students presented their selections, the works were passed around for gentle, careful examination.

After all the students had shared their selections, I put up the term "Gift Books" on the chalkboard. I told the students that these books were often packaged in these special formats and sizes to be given as special gifts. Then I asked them, based on our sharing in class, to list the key qualities of "Gift Books."

Among those they identified were

- Unusual size—oversized or undersized.
- Many richly colored illustrations (I supplied the vocabulary phrase "profusely illustrated").
- Selection, compilation, or editing of famous writer's works or famous artist's creations.
- Shiny paper/special paper (I supplied the phrase "paper stock").
- Excerpts, quotes, and poetry from famous writers.
- Beautiful art/photo prints.
- A mix of different print (I supplied the term "typefaces").
- A gimmick or three-dimensional component.
- Special cloth, silver, even jeweled bindings.

I asked the students if they personally would be pleased to own some of the beautiful volumes they had borrowed. They all nodded emphatically. Then I revealed that as a result of their initial interest and extensive research in beautiful gift books, we were going to create our own beautiful volumes as gifts for our friends and families.

"But we're not famous writers or great artists," said Felix.

"You don't have to be famous to *publish* a gift volume. You choose what's in it. You don't have to create it. You just have to have good taste and design ideas," countered Ramon.

"Right," I said. Then I distributed the "Give the Gift of Family Literacy" worksheet (see Section III, Worksheet 17) and told the students they would have a week to come up with a concept and a text or photocopied set of art prints/photographs they wanted to use for their "gift volume" (being careful about copyrights). Although I told them they could work in pairs, I stipulated that each individual would create his own gift volume. As an added motivation for the students, I assured them that if they were successful in their efforts, we would hold a "Gift Book" publishing party for them and the designated recipients of the volumes.

During the week that elapsed between our introductory session and our first design workshop, several students saw me privately with relevant questions, which I later shared with the class. Among these were:

- Should the volume be designed to fit the interests of the recipient? (Yes!)
- Should I talk to the person in my family

or the friend I want to give the book to, to feel out their interests? (Yes!)

• Will you give us the binding materials, copies, and a choice of paper? (Yes!)

• Can we use desktop publishing and the drawing software in the lab? (Yes!)

• May I bring in my own wrapping paper and cloth material and wallpaper samples? (Yes!)

When the day came for sharing the student-generated gift book concepts, the students' excitement was almost palpable. Again, although my expectations were high given the interest they had displayed throughout, their concepts far exceeded what I had imagined they would plan. First, I was surprised by the breadth of their literary text selections. These ran the spectrum from the works of Dr. Seuss, Judy Blume, E.B. White, John Czescka, Shel Silverstein, and Ann Martin to Shakespeare, Dereck Wolcott, Robert Browning, W.B. Yeats, and Isaac Bashevis Singer. When I asked the students how they had come up with such adult authors, they explained that they had discussed the selections with their parents, grandparents, and other adults for whom they wanted to design gift books. One student was creating a special book for an elderly person she worked with in an after-school program at a nursing home. Her friend loved the stories of Isaac Bashevis Singer, so she had found some of his books in the library.

Second, although our budget was insufficient to help all of my budding gift book designers precisely realize their elaborate goals, we were able to provide the students with enough paper, binding materials, foils, and access to copying facilities to allow them to realize their designs on a fairly high scale. Moreover, other knowledgeable adults enriched our project. Our school arts specialist led a full two-and-a-half-hour session in bookbinding. A publisher I called on a whim sent us a special projects editor, who gave the students some insights into the way publishing firms decide on, price, and market gift books. The computer specialist graciously provided access to the lab and technical assistance for the desktop publishers. Work on production spanned four in-class periods, as well as student-requested lunch and after-school time.

Finally, the students created invitations for the gift book recipients and elaborately wrapped their "Gifts of Literacy." The high point of this extremely satisfying skills-in-use project was our "Gifts of Literacy" reception for student publishers and recipients. We held it on a weekend morning so parents and family members who worked could come to get their student-designed gift books. Even so, not every recipient was able to come; but the delight, excitement, gratitude, and warmth exuded by the recipients who did come filled all of us—teachers, specialists, and students—with pride. One parent rushed over to tell me with tears in her eyes that this present was doubly meaningful to her because she could never get her son to read and he had never talked with her about what she read.

The special projects editor offered to fund the project the next year and invite the students to a design studio so they could gain more professional insights into the gift book process.

But the best gift of the day and outcome of the project, as far as I was concerned, came from one of my students who prior to the project "didn't care much for reading." He came over to thank me for letting the class pilot the project:

> You know, I'm reading some of that Twain stuff my grandfather likes. Twain is very good, once you get past the dialect. From now on, I'm going to make gift books every year for special people. I'm going to read more to find good writers whose work I can use.

And I vowed to provide my students with continued opportunities to give and receive the gift of family literacy.

⟡   ⟡   ⟡

Teacher to Teacher

You certainly have given me plenty of strategies for evolving the multicultural classroom. But what do I do when I run out of the adaptable strategies outlined here? How do I customize your strategies to meet the unique needs of my students? What about parents, families, the school community, and the neighborhood? How do I make certain that they add their perspectives in evolving the multicultural classroom?

This question is very pertinent to the challenge of *evolving* the multicultural classroom. None of the strategies or activities is static, and I hope that the strategies and resources in this book will serve to inspire your own evolving multicultural classroom.

Included in Section III are specific "Parent Participation" worksheets that can be used as models to draw parents in as partners and collaborators. These worksheets, as well as the other worksheets, "Teaching Modules," and other resources in Section III, will not only be useful in their printed formats, but will serve to inspire students, parents, community members, and teachers to initiate other multicultural classroom activities.

References

Baker, G.C. (1994). *Planning and Organizing for Multicultural Instruction*. 2nd ed. Menlo Park, Calif.: Addison-Wesley.

Banks, J.A. (1991). *Teaching Strategies for Ethnic Studies*. 5th ed. Boston: Allyn and Bacon.

Belles Lettres. (1989). New York: Stewart, Tabori & Chang Inc. (Address: 740 Broadway, New York, NY 10003).

Gardner, H. (1983). *Frames of Mind*. New York: Basic Books.

Gardner, H. (1991). *The Unschooled Mind*. New York: Basic Books.

Gardner, H. (1993). *Multiple Intelligences*. New York: Basic Books.

Schuman, J.A. (1980). *Art from Many Hands: Multicultural Art Projects for Home and School*. Englewood Cliffs, N.J.: Prentice Hall.

SECTION III

RESOURCES

Worksheet 1. Under the Multicultural Umbrella

NAME _____ DATE _____

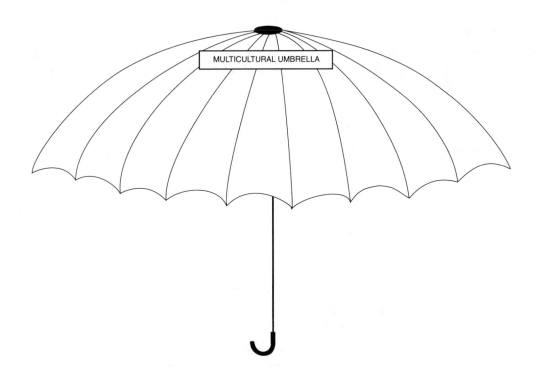

MULTICULTURAL UMBRELLA

Questions to Ponder:

Who is included? Groups of various individuals from different ethnic, racial, religious, special needs, special concerns backgrounds.

If an individual is grouped under one of these categories, can he or she "belong" to only one group?

Criteria for inclusion under the umbrella:

• Victim of discrimination, bias, prejudice, scapegoating.

• In need of social, legislative, medical, or educational equity.

Worksheet 2. What Is Multiculturalism?

NAME _____ DATE _____

Note: This survey was prepared for parents and teachers but may be adapted for use with middle school students.

Use this as a "pre" or "post" litmus test of your perspectives on Multicultural Education and Multicultural Classroom Approaches. When we conclude our study, you'll write your own evaluation on the *extent* to which your views have *changed,* as well as which strategies or ideas changed them.

You will keep one copy of this "pre" survey for yourself and hand in one copy (without your name), so be as detailed and as honest as you wish. The more detail on the "pre" survey, the better you'll be able to evaluate any changes or lack of same in the "post" survey.

Step 1

Draw or write any images, words, or responses that come to mind as you ponder. Make a "Web" or draw, if you like.

MATERIALS FOR A DIVERSE CLASSROOM
MULTICULTURAL EDUCATION

DIVERSITY - MULTICULTURAL

Step 2

Fill in the following. Be honest: no one but you will "know" what you said.

1. My initial "gut" response to my child learning "Multicultural understandings" or "diversity" or "tolerance" in the classroom is:

2. Multicultural Education is _____

                isn't _____

another "add on" to the curriculum.

3. Multicultural Education is _____

                isn't _____

for ethnically diverse students only because:

4. Multicultural Education is _____

                isn't _____

good for my child because:

5. Multicultural courses or units should _____

              should not _____

be taught by white persons who lack color and are Protestants since:

6. Do you agree or disagree? Explain why or why not.

"In order to infuse Multicultural understanding in my basic reading, writing, and mathematics curricula, I have to get special Multicultural materials. To properly teach Multicultural Education, I need training and on-site support."

7. "I believe that exploring alternative lifestyles (including gays and lesbians) and families, as well as detailing handicapping conditions and discrimination against AIDS sufferers, is not appropriate for discussion in grades K to 3,

1) but can be initiated in grade 4   _____

2) can be initiated in grade 6   _____

3) should never be discussed in class   _____

    or

4)   _____

    I feel that:

8. As far as I am concerned, Multicultural Issues and Education are:

_____ a "buzzword" of the '90s that will fade to be replaced by another word.

_____ a necessary approach to education for citizenship in our diverse society.

_____ more necessary for troubled racially tense schools and neighborhoods than for more stable communities.

_____ an "overhyped" movement that is too controversial.

9. I personally feel:

_____ uncomfortable with discussion of intergroup tensions, cultural or racial issues.

_____ unprepared for these potentially "difficult" talks.

_____ disconnected from these issues

_____ committed to working for intergroup understandings.

As a citizen of _____, I feel Multicultural Education is:

Worksheet 3. Naming Our Cultural Selves

NAME _____   CLASS _____   DATE _____

You are cordially invited to . . .

"The Naming of Our Cultural Selves"

Credit for the language of this invitation goes to the poet T. S. Eliot's "The Naming of Cats."

Write or draw (or both) as detailed a reaction to each of these "name" invitations as you wish or can do . . .

1. "The name that the family use daily. . . sensible everyday names"

   (Include names in English, nicknames, cultural/foreign language, native language, affectionate names)

2. "A name that's particular . . . more dignified"

   (What you're called at school or in the outside world by friends and by strangers)

3. What you call or think of yourself as your . . . "ineffable effable . . . singular name"

   (Include name in English and personal cultural/foreign language nickname)

Worksheet 4. First Day of School Oral Histories

NAME _____ **CLASS** _____ **DATE** _____

How old were you when you started school?

What did your classroom look like?

Were you afraid to go to school? Why?

What happened when you got into school?

Was the teacher nice?

Did you get hurt by the other kids? Did you get hit by other kids?

Did you cry? Why?

Were you afraid nobody would come for you?

What did you do in school?

Did you get to go to the bathroom?

Did you ever have an accident in class?

Did the kids make fun of you?

Did you like school when you first got there?

Did you like it later?

Worksheet 5. F.A.L.L. Into Literature—First Line Follow Through

NAME _____ **CLASS** _____ **DATE** _____

Instructions: The following are the first lines from seven famous books. Read them through first and list any questions or reaction you have to them.

1. "Serene was a word you could put to Brooklyn, New York."

   Questions/Reaction _____

   _____

2. "Early in the spring of 1750, in the village of Juffure, four days upriver from the coast of the Gambia, West Africa, a man-child was born to Omoro and Binta Kinte."

   _____

   _____

3. "Somewhere a child began to cry."

   _____

   _____

4. "Now she sits alone and remembers."

   _____

   _____

5. "The law, as quoted, lays down a fair conduct of life, and one not easy to follow."

   _____

   _____

6. "I look at myself in the mirror."

   _____

   _____

7. "José Palacios, his oldest servant, found him floating naked with his eyes open in the purifying waters of his bath and thought he had drowned."

   _____

   _____

Now select the one that touches you most and write a "First Line, Follow Through" that picks up on the plot/end suggested to you.

Worksheet 6. Storyboarding Reader Response

Name: _____

STORYBOARD   Title: _____

Worksheet 7. Cresting for Character and Community

Teacher's Instructions

1. Set up two computer stations for two to three students apiece. On one station, install drawing software; on the adjacent one, word processing software. Select one literary work that can serve as your multicultural literature focus. Within that work, choose an excerpt that's usually evocative, both verbally and visually. Read the excerpt twice, but *leave out the specific words that identify the country of origin*. Ask your student listeners to fill in blank crests, shields, or circles with pictures or words signifying the book character's concerns—by hand or through a computer drawing program. Students can work individually or in teams.

2. After your initial reading, hand out the duplicated excerpts to the students or have them open their own book copies (if they have the books) to the passage. Allow the students enough time to review the passage on their own and to add additional details to their character's crests or circles. Ask that students write in their word-processing files what countries or ethnic background the main character comes from. Give the students a chance to share and discuss their ideas about the country or ethnicity of the main character. List their ideas and show them on a large monitor or projection screen.

3. After students have had sufficient time to complete the activity, ask them to print out their crests. Then give them time to explicate the ways in which their graphics depict various values.

4. As the students share these values, list them on a large monitor, to be printed out later for a Multicultural Computer Crest Expo. Students also can examine and discuss the similarities and differences among the crests created, using the same drawing program based on the reading.

5. After the students identify the values and issues of the literature, ask them which of these concerns are "common" to everyone and which ones "uniquely reflect the particular culture" the literature details. Give them time to reflect on these questions and enter their ideas in their files.

6. After the students identify and discuss the "common" themes in the literature, ask them to focus on the "unique" or "culture specific" features of the text.

Cresting Forms

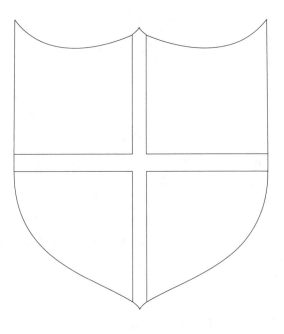

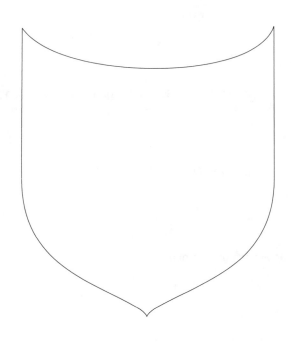

Worksheet 8. Showing Peer Portraits

NAME _____ CLASS _____ DATE _____

Choose one of the following:

a. Write an acrostic poem about yourself or a peer. For example:

Nancy is Italian

American Catholic

New York

Camaro sports car

Young woman's greatest love in her family.

b. Inverted literary technique: write a letter to a friend about a person, as if you have just met him or her.

c. Write a personal ad about yourself or a peer.

d. List three quotes your chosen peer is always saying.

e. Draw a cartoon of the person and place a bubble over his or her head, showing possible sayings.

f. Create a mixed graphic/visual art portrait of peer.

g. Design an evocative computer arts graphic of peer.

Worksheet 9. Showing Peer Portraits in Literature

NAME _____ **CLASS** _____ **DATE** _____

Pick out main character of book, TV show, comic character, movies, and three quotes from this character.

Don't tell anyone the character you've done. Draw a picture of the character, if you wish.

List three quotes character is always saying.

_____

_____

_____

Write a description of this person.

Worksheet 10. Peer Portrait—Multicultural Perspectives

NAME _____ **CLASS** _____ **DATE** _____

Background (Country, Religion, Neighborhood, Ethnic):

List as many items as you can:

Of the above, I most identify myself as:

Likes: (Foods, Fashion, Music, Films, Books, Television)

Dislikes: (See above _____)

Nightmares, Fears (Self, Ethnic Group)

Wishes, Hopes, Dreams (Self, Ethnic Group)

I care deeply about:

Worksheet 11. Cultural Collages: Multicultural Awareness Newspaper Investigation

NAME _____ **CLASS** _____ **DATE** _____

Date of Newspapers Surveyed _____ Newspapers Used _____

_____

I. Analysis/Survey

As you go through the newspaper, list all references to the target ethnic or cultural groups by news section, classification (story, ad, graphic, photo) and by effect (positive, negative, neutral).

Target Group: _____

II. References

	News Section	Classification	Effect
1.			
2.			
3.			
4.			
5.			
6.			
7.			
8.			
9.			
10.			

III. Evaluation

Based on this date's survey, I find that the coverage of my target group is:

_____ valid

_____ perpetuates a favorable stereotype

_____ perpetuates a negative stereotype

_____ provides insufficient data to make a statement

_____ My reaction to my findings is:

I would like to see coverage of this target group:

_____ changed

_____ remain the same

_____ stopped

because:

IV. Cultural Collage Example

This collage was produced by Mark Gura for use in various teacher/student workshops around this strategy and others. Reproduced by permission.

Worksheet 12. Pop Up Manila Folders

Materials:
Glue, file folders, scissors, markers

Instructions:
As file folder lies closed, cut a square as indicated:

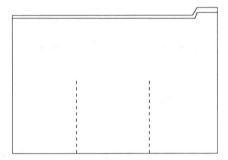

Next, open file folder, push up, and "pop out" your "pop-up" pouch

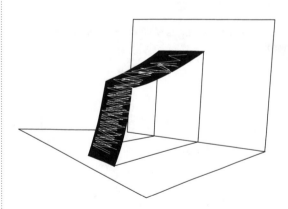

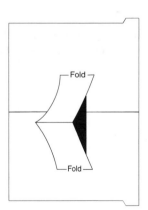

Cut and paste newspaper pictures or headlines on Pop-up section.

Cut and paste news text on sides.

Add graphics or designs as desired.

Hinge up additional pictures using cut manila file folder strips.

Worksheet 13. Hero Rites—Talking, Writing, and Thinking About Heroes

NAME _____ **CLASS** _____ **DATE** _____

List those individuals who you feel are your heroes:

Look at your list—what qualities or actions or statements made you put someone on your list?

Complete: A hero to me is someone who:

_____

_____

Heroic Outreach—Talking about and sharing our heroes.

Pick three individuals not in our class. Try to get at least two adults of different ages. Ask them to name their heroes and tell why they consider each of these individuals a hero . . .

Worksheet 14. Family F.I.N.D. Newspaper Journal

NAME _____ CLASS _____ DATE _____

Newspaper Used _____

Family Members _____

_____

_____

Adult Family Member   **Student**

_____   _____

Tell Me: What Is It?

I don't understand this word, graphic, item (clip and paste if you like)

                                                                Family Response:

_____

What do you think about? . . .   What do you think about?

How do you react to?   How do you react to?

Can we: go here, do this, buy this, try this

(Paste offerings, opportunities from newspaper here . . .)

_____

Isn't this terrible?   Isn't this terrific?

   Newspaper Reader Response, Reaction

_____

Predicting probable story, events in the next week, we'll read:

Worksheet 15. Cultural Greeting Cards

NAME _____ **CLASS** _____ **DATE** _____

Instructions for Teacher:

This is a multidisciplinary research project for elementary and middle school students that promotes intergroup respect.

I.   Ask students to identify a seasonal celebration particular to their cultural or ethnic or religious background.

II.   Have students tell or write about the celebration. Ask them to include the following if they can:

- Name of celebration, background (why/how/where was it originally celebrated)
- Customs/rituals (what you do on this celebration)
- Gifts (kinds)
- Songs/sayings that go with the celebration (in native language and then translation)

III.   Give students a chance to share information on their celebration.

IV.   Then tell students that one of the major national card companies has decided to produce a line of cultural greeting cards. Ask them to design a greeting card for their cultural celebration.

Discuss or identify the following Greeting Card elements to be included in the student creations:

1. Opening card design—Illustration, salutation, colors, etc.

2. Message inside (foreign language/saying)—Optional: illustration

3. Back of card: Name of designer/company, city, state; name/theme of card line.

V.   Students can share their designs or exhibit them or use a computer program to mass-produce them (i.e., Broderbund *Printshop Deluxe/KIDS CUTS*) variations on Cultural Card Greetings.

1. Parents and children can create "authentic" greeting cards together.

2. Parents/community members can serve as on-site classroom consultants during the process.

3. Students/parents can critique and "correct" current "authentic" commercial cultural greeting cards (found in stationery stores).

4. Parents/students can respond/react to "Mixed Blessing" type greeting cards that purposely mix two or more cultures together to show intergroup respect.

5. Students can research cultures other than their own and create cards for them.

Worksheet 16. Fortune Cookie Critics

Reactions and Reflections

NAME _____ CLASS _____ DATE _____

My fortune says (copy or paste saying)_____
_____

This saying means (write it down using your own words)

_____
_____
_____

I agree/disagree with it because

_____
_____
_____

I think this saying "applies" as "appropriate" for me because

_____
_____
_____

If you think about it, this saying could apply to anyone because

_____
_____
_____

This saying will help sell more Chinese food because it makes the reader (eater) feel

_____

_____

_____

On the other hand, it might not be good for the reader (eater) to accept it without thinking because it could make him or her

_____

_____

_____

Fortune Cookie Fun Follow Throughs . . .

I think the author of this fortune earns his/her living by day as a (name a profession) because

_____

_____

_____

If I were hired to write sayings for fortune cookies, here are some I'd write:

1. _____

2. _____

3. _____

4. _____

5. _____

My ideal fortune cookie design would look like:

   draw it

The best fortune I ever got read

_____

_____

_____

My favorite fortune cookie looks_____

and tastes_____.

Worksheet 17. Gifts of Literacy

Individual Concept Sheet and Gift Book Planner

NAME _____ **CLASS** _____ **DATE** _____

Gift Recipient's Name _____ Age _____

Adult _____

Child _____

Friend _____

Gift Recipient's Favorite Author _____

Favorite Work by that Author _____

Gift Book Concept (check appropriate one or write out your own idea)

_____ oversized

_____ undersized

_____ other (explain)

Literary Gift Book   **Art Gift Book**

_____ Selected Author   _____ Selected Artist

The book will contain:

_____ Excerpts from the   _____ Photocopies, postcards, prints of
author's work(s)   artist's work

_____ Quotes from the author

_____ A poem or short story   _____ Artist's life
by the author

_____ Several authors on the theme of   _____ Pop-up Book

_____   _____ Pull-out Book

Special Art Supplies/Materials I'll need in addition to regular bookbinding materials:

_____ Cloth/brocade/velvet   _____ Paints (watercolor)

_____ Goldleaf paper   _____ markers   _____ pastels   _____ ink

Other: _____

I need access to:

_____ computer lab

_____ the library

_____ photocopy machine

Module 1. Making Core Curriculum Connections—Felita

NAME _____ **CLASS** _____ **DATE** _____

Text: Nicholasa Mohr, *Felita* (New York: Barton, Skylark, 1979).

I. Ten Key Multicultural Concepts:

1. Change
2. Citizenship
3. Culture
4. Empathy
5. Environment

6. Identity
7. Interdependence
8. Nation/State
9. Scarcity
10. Technology

II. Literature-Based Activities

1. Geographic Graphics:

(Link to key concepts—Identity, Environment, Empathy)

Make "Connections" by copying down all the words in the book (or selected passage) that provide information about site-specific weather, vegetation, climate, and sense data. List the character who supplies the data.

_____ , _____ , _____   _____

_____ , _____ , _____   _____

_____ , _____ , _____   _____

2. Geographic Graphics:

(Link to key concepts—Environment, Change)

Now take a passage—48–50 words—and "draw it" out:

III. Writing/Research:

(Link to key concepts—Empathy, Identity)

1. Felita is writing a letter to Mami and Papi about her trip to Puerto Rico. Find out: what places she might visit in Puerto Rico, what the climate would be like, what the resources, products, and cultural life are like.

2. Felita keeps a diary of her feelings about the move from the old neighborhood. Write some sample entries.

IV. Research:

(Link to recommended key concepts—Environment)

1. Find out about the flowers and climate of Puerto Rico.

2. Fill in the major sites on a blank map of Puerto Rico.

V. Mathematics:

1. How much would it cost for Tito Jorge and Felita to visit Puerto Rico now? _____

2. Get some travel brochures to help them plan their trip. _____

VI. Family Values:

For Mami, Papi, Tito, Johnny, and Abuelita (Link to recommended concepts—Culture, Empathy, Interdependence, Citizenship)

1. List quotes or details from the book that tell about family values.

Example: "Friendship is one of the best things in this whole world."—Abuelita

"I knew I would always think of her [Abuelita . . the deceased grandmother]."—Felita

"It's for better schools. You children will thank us."—Papi

VII. Gap Generation:

(Link to Semiotics—Reader Response Theory)

What questions can you generate about these areas? (What else do you want to know?) Ask about characters, events that went before/events that came after.

1. _____

2. _____

3. _____

4. _____

5. _____

6. _____

7. _____

8. _____

VIII. "Story Sequeways"

(Creative Writing, Critical Thinking)

1. Before the story began (Prequel):

2. After the story ended (Sequel):

3. Other stories still unwritten:

4. Another character mentioned but not met in the book was _____.

He (or she) feels_____.

While the events in this story are going on/or before the events in this story went on/or after the events in this story, he (or she)

_____ .

_____ .

IX. Take an "Artful" Angle

1. Visit a craft museum or get a book featuring "Puerto Rican" arts. Tell about it.

2. Get a recipe for "flan" (Spanish egg custard). Copy/draw it.

X. Evolve a "Puerto Rican" dictionary:

(Cultural phrases based on *Felita*)

Begin with:

      bodega:

      dulce de coco:

      mihijita:

      que pasa:

      por dios:

Module 1a. "Bubble" Your Way to Character Study

NAME _____CLASS _____DATE _____

Title of Book _____ Author: _____

List the key characters:

1 _____   2 _____

3 _____   4 _____

Instructions: For each character listed above, copy as many key quotes (things the character actually says or things that are said about him or her) as you can. Fill the top part of the character bubble with them.

Then fill the bottom part of the character bubble with physical or personality descriptions of the character copied from the book.

Get as many as you can. If you feel like it, draw a picture of your character underneath the bubble. Fill up as many worksheets as there are key characters.

Quotes:

_____

_____

_____

_____

_____

Character's name   Description

_____   _____

Module 1b. Beginnings and Endings . . .

NAME _____CLASS _____DATE_____

Drawing a Picture-Based Plot Design:

Draw a picture of the first page or pages of the story

Picture 1—The Beginning

Picture 2—You Predict the Ending

Take a look at your pictures . . .

Now WITHOUT READING THE BOOK, predict what you think happens in the *middle* of the book . . .

You can draw pictures of it as well if you like.

Picture 3—You Predict the Middle

Now read the book. After you complete it, reread your predictions. How accurate were you? Where did you go wrong?

If you went wrong, was your middle "good" as a story on its own?

Module 2. Making Core Curriculum Connections—Sarah, Plain and Tall

NAME _____ CLASS _____ DATE _____

Text: Patricia Machachlan, *Sarah, Plain and Tall* (New York: Harper, 1985).

I. Ten Key Multicultural Concepts:

1. Change
2. Citizenship
3. Culture
4. Empathy
5. Environment

6. Identity
7. Interdependence
8. Nation/State
9. Scarcity
10. Technology

II. Literature-Based Activities

1. Geographic Connections:

(Link to key concepts—Identity, Environment, Empathy).

Make "Connections" by copying down all the words in the book (or selected) passage that provide information about site-specific weather, vegetation, climate and sense data. List the character who supplies the data.

_____ , _____ , _____   _____

_____ , _____ , _____   _____

_____ , _____ , _____   _____

2. Geographic Graphics:

(Link to key concepts—Environment, Change)

Now take a passage—48–50 words—and "draw it" out

3. **Writing:**

(Link to key concepts—Empathy, Identity)

Sarah is writing home to her brother William about Pa, Anna, and Caleb. Complete her letter.

    Dear William,

                                    Love,

                                    Sarah

4. **Research:** (Link to recommended key concepts (Environment)

Compare and contrast the climate of Maine with the prairie climate.

_____

_____

_____

_____

II. Science: Botany

List the kinds of flowers that grow on the prairie.

_____

_____

List those that grow in Maine.

_____

_____

III. Family Life in the Prairie Days:

(Link to recommended concepts—Culture, Empathy, Interdependence, Citizenship)

List details about school life, home responsibilities, customs, and civic life from the book:

1. _____   5. _____

2. _____   6. _____

3. _____   7. _____

4. _____

IV. Gap Generation:

(Semiotics—Reader Response Theory)

What questions can you generate about these areas? (What else do you want to know?) Ask about characters, events that went before/ events that came after.

1. _____

2. _____

3. _____

4. _____

5. _____

6. _____

7. _____

8. _____

V. "Story Sequeways"

(Creative Writing, Critical Thinking)

1. Before the story began (Prequel):

2. After the story ended (Sequel):

3. Other stories still unwritten:

4. Another character mentioned but not met in the book was _____.

He (or she) feels_____.

While the events in this story are going on/or before the events in this story went on/or after the events in this story, he (or she)

_____.

_____.

VI. Take an "Artful" Angle

1. Visit a craft museum or get a book featuring Prairie-inspired designs, quilts, clothes. Draw some of these if you wish.

2. Get recordings of Sarah's songs and music of the times.

List:

_____   _____

_____   _____

_____   _____

Module 3. "Responsibilities" and "Values"

Module 3a. Reading the "News" for "Responsibility" and "Values"

NAME_____CLASS _____DATE _____

1. As you read the news, cut out words/headlines or pictures that discuss or show events, trends, people or movements that you "admire" or that "bother" you.

Paste or glue here

For each item, tell why you "admire" it or are "bothered" by it

1. _____

1. _____

2. _____

2. _____

3. _____

3. _____

4. _____

4. _____

5. _____

5. _____

6. _____

6. _____

2. Look at the items you selected. Circle all the words that are "Responsibility" or "Value" words.

Module 3b. Bill of Responsibilities—Cases to Consider

Note to teacher: These are sample cases that one group of students listed. Each class or group of students should list cases currently in the news.

1. Should Cabinet officers be completely law abiding? If child care—getting a perfect match for your child—conflicts with the immigration law, what do you do?

2. Case of Katie Beers—What are the responsibilities of neighbors, friends, storekeepers, media, school, etc.?

3. Case of Amy Fisher—How current should the media keep this affair current?

4. Transplant Ethics—How should we place fetuses on transplant waiting list? Is the policy of early listing on the list, to guarantee transplant, the most viable for success? Should waiting time be the criterion for allocating organs? Is it really impartial?

5. Baboon Liver—Should doctors perform this transplant on patients who sign up for it?

6. Doctors admit ignoring dying patients' wishes with unwanted treatment and inadequate pain relief.

7. Passive Smoke—Class A Carcinogenic—How responsible are we?

8. Right to Die—Does a patient have the right to do so? May Dr. Kevorkian assist him?

9. Woe to Zoe—To what extent must we hold a public official "responsible" for obeying all the laws? Does this need a new tenet of law?

10. What are we "responsible" to do when members of New Jersey Rider College's Phi Kappa PSI hold a racist hazing event?

Module 3c. Social Action Reactions

NAME _____CLASS _____DATE _____

As I read the news today, I felt that as a reader and a citizen
I could (should):

I am a student, but I feel that adults in my community (the world) have the power or responsibility to:

As a student, I can help by_____.

When I am an adult member of society, I will work to see that _____

never happens, but that more_____

are developed and supported.

Module 3d. "Valley Forge" Sample Bill of Responsibility

Preamble. *Freedom and responsibility are mutual and inseparable: we can ensure enjoyment of the one only by exercising the other. Freedom for all of us depends on responsibility by each of us. To secure and expand our liberties, therefore, we accept these responsibilities as individual members of a free society:*

To be fully responsible for our own actions and for the consequences of those actions. Freedom to choose carries with it the responsibility for our choices.

To respect the rights and beliefs of others. In a free society, diversity flourishes. Courtesy and consideration toward others are measures of a civilized society.

To give sympathy, understanding and help to others. As we hope others will help us when we are in need, we should help others when they are in need.

To do our best to meet our own and our families' needs. There is no personal freedom without economic freedom. By helping ourselves and those closest to us to become productive members of society, we contribute to the strength of the nation.

To respect and obey the laws. Laws are mutually accepted rules by which, together, we maintain a free society. Liberty itself is built on a foundation of law. That foundation provides an orderly process for changing laws. It also depends on our obeying laws once they have been freely adopted.

To respect the property of others, both private and public. No one has a right to what is not his or hers. The right to enjoy what is ours depends on our respecting the right of others to enjoy what is theirs.

To share with others our appreciation of the benefits and obligations of freedom. Freedom shared is freedom strengthened.

To participate constructively in the nation's political life. Democracy depends on an active citizenry. It depends equally on an informed citizenry.

To help freedom survive by assuming personal responsibility for its defense. Our nation cannot survive unless we defend it. Its security rests on the individual determination of each of us to help preserve it.

To respect the rights and to meet the responsibilities on which our liberty rests and our democracy depends. This is the essence of freedom. Maintaining it requires our common effort, all together and each individually.

Module 3e. Bill of Responsibilities—Form

NAME _____CLASS _____DATE _____

Preamble:

Introduction—Why this Bill of Responsibilities is needed. Who are the authors? What caused it to be written (newspaper headlines, issues, community problems)? What connection, if any, do *Responsibilities* have with *Rights*?) Write a Preamble here.

_____

_____

_____

Therefore we (I) accept these Responsibilities as individual members of _____
(school, community, neighborhood, organization, etc.)

Responsibilities:

(You may wish to "draw" your responsibilities on the side of your "Bill" or create a "Drawn" Bill of Responsibilities.)

TO _____

TO _____

TO _____

TO _____

TO _____

TO _____

Module 4. Mayoral Family F.I.N.D. (Families Involved in Newspaper Discovery)

Module 4a. Newspaper Discovery—Family Learning Scrapbook

Purpose:

- To involve students and families in targeted news family learning activities
- To provide students with an introduction to format journals
- To engage students, teachers and families in ongoing discussion and analysis of the mayoral campaign

Suggested Materials:

- Glue sticks/glue
- Markers
- Scissors
- Crayons
- New York *Newsday*
- Note Home to Parents
- Mayoral Family F.I.N.D. Worksheet Packets (at least 7–14 copies of the worksheet per student)

Optional:

8 X 11-in. poster board/or cut down files with holes punched on the left

Ribbon to tie the scrapbook

- Students and parents might bring in and create their own journals.
- For younger grades, the final journals could also be Mayoral Family F.I.N.D. Big Book Formats.

Preorganizing Activity:

- Invite parents/family members to class for an Introductory Mayoral Focus, Newspapers in Education Exploration workshop.
- Engage them in looking through the newspapers and cutting out headlines, photos, and graphics that interest them as families.
- Provide time for both the parents and children to clip, share, and discuss news items that interest them.

Procedure:

1. Tell students and parents/family members that they will be involved in focusing as family teams on the Mayoral Campaign as it is covered in the newspaper. Their joint family endeavor will be called Project Mayoral Family F.I.N.D.—Families Involved in Newspaper Discovery.

2. Distribute the Mayoral Family F.I.N.D. worksheets (Modules 4a and 4b) to the family teams. Give them time to go through the sheets and ask any questions about the format or instructions.

3. Have the teams go through the newspapers on their first Mayoral Family F.I.N.D. expedition. Pass out poster board for them to put together the first page of their Family Learning Scrapbook.

4. After the family teams have compiled the first pages of their scrapbooks, give them a chance to show these to the class as a whole.

5. Direct the teams to focus on the "What's next?" prediction section of the page. Have each team make a prediction about events in the campaign for the following week. List these predictions on a large experiential chart.

_____

_____

Further Activities:

- Maintain charts of Family F.I.N.D. Mayoral Campaign predictions. Check/confirm these predictions against the actual campaign events.

- As the campaign draws to a close, a Mayoral Family F.I.N.D. Festival can be held with the PTA and community as participants. Family teams can show highlights from their scrapbooks and discuss their predictions.

- Mayoral Family F.I.N.D. teams of parents and children can present their Mayoral Family F.I.N.D. scrapbooks at a PTA meeting or to another class of potential family members so they too can set up a Mayoral Family F.I.N.D. shared newspaper learning project.

- Big Books can be created to include a specific question, issue, or candidate.

Performance Objectives:

Students will be able to:

_____

_____

_____

Language Arts:

- Critically read for and isolate pertinent items, using a set format

- Formulate decisions and take pro and con positions on issues

- Generate thoughtful questions based on independent reading

- Develop and articulate (in writing and speech) their reactions to the news

- Maintain a sequenced record of the unfolding of the campaign

- Read, clip, and analyze pertinent graphics, news articles, letters, and columns

- Share newsreading experiences and responses with their parents

Critical Thinking:

- Work with visual imagery
- Develop a point of view or a conclusion, articulate it, and defend it
- Predict outcomes
- Check and confirm predictions
- Generate questions and explore responses to them
- Take notes and record data:

_____

_____

Module 4b. Newspaper Discovery—Family Journal

NAME _____CLASS _____DATE _____

Parent _____Child _____

Newspapers Read/Used: _____

Target/Topic: Mayoral Campaign . . .

Tell Me . . . (Unfamiliar Vocabulary . . .
Things I've never heard of from the past . . . Names I don't know)
                    Child   **Parent (Family Member)**

What is it? Phrases . . . New terms or trends . . . Paste in if you like
                    Child   **Parent (Family Member)**

What do you think? Questions raised by the news—I'd like to know what you think . . .
                    Child   **Parent (Family Member)**

Candidate Comments/Statements about the candidate:

Do you agree?   Disagree?   How do you react?
                    Child   **Paren**t

Mayoral News Reader Reaction
How do you feel about what you read?
"Isn't that terrible? Isn't this terrific? How interesting!"
Paste in graphics, headlines, or cartoons that illustrate your point.
                    Child   **Parent**

NEXT!!—In a few days, the Mayoral Campaign news item I listed or news story I clipped will have evolved to . . .
                    Child   **Parent**

Sample Letter

Dear Parent,

I am evolving a Multicultural classroom environment as part of our course/study. To make certain that this Multicultural classroom reflects your values and needs, I invite you to a parent planning meeting on:

Date   _____

Time   _____

Place   _____

I look forward to your assistance, support, and collaboration in this vital endeavor.

Please feel free to contact me with any ideas or suggestions you have for the meeting.

Thank you,

_____

(Teacher)

Pre/Post Assessment

Dear Parent,

Enclosed are two Pre/Post Assessment Forms ("What Is Multiculturalism?") for evolving the multicultural classroom. Please fill them both out in as much detail as you can. Return one to me unsigned, and keep the other for your own records.

When the school year (term) ends, you will get two copies of the same assessment to do again. One of these will be returned to me, and you will compare and contrast your own copy to your preassessment so you can determine what changes, if any, there have been in your preassessment of Multicultural Education.

Thank you,

_____

(Teacher)

[Note to teacher: Attach two copies of Worksheet 2, "What Is Multiculturalism?" in Section III.]

One of the positive outcomes of the growth of multicultural education is the plethora of excellent multicultural anthologies and bibliographies available. The following sections list anthologies, bibliographies, and other resources that were particularly useful in piloting the strategies for evolving the multicultural classroom. All references are to the editions that I have used in my classrooms and workshops.

Selected Multicultural Literature Anthologies

Allen, P.G., ed. (1989). *Spider Woman's Granddaughters: Traditional Tales and Contemporary Writing by Native American Women*. Boston: Beacon Press.

Baven, H., ed. (1991). *In the Beginning—Great First Lines from Your Favorite Books*. San Francisco: Chronicle Books.

Chin, F., J. Chan, P. Chan, L.F. Inada, and S. Hsu Wong, eds. (1983). *Aiiieeeee! An Anthology of Asian-American Writings*. Washington, D.C.: Howard University Press.

Cohn, A.L., ed. (1993). *From Sea to Shining Sea—A Treasury of American Folklore and Folksongs*. New York: Scholastic. Includes songs and sayings, with selections from various cultural strands, including Portuguese, Mexican, Chinese, American, African American, Norwegian, Cajun, Cherokee, Jewish.

Gallo, D., ed. (1994). *Join In—Multiethnic Short Stories by Outstanding Writers for Young Adults*. New York: Delacourte Press. Stories featuring American teenagers from diverse cultural groups; includes stories about Vietnamese, Puerto Rican, Cambodian, Japanese, Cuban, Lebanese, Black, Laotian, Chicano, and Pueblo Indian teenagers.

Lass, A.H. (1969). *21 Great Stories*. 2nd ed. New York: Mentor. Includes *The Pearl* by John Steinbeck.

McMillan, T., ed. (1990). *Breaking Ice: An Anthology of Contemporary African-American Fiction*. New York: Anchor Books. Includes works by Paule Marschall, Alice Walker, John Edgar Wideman, and Ishmael Reed.

Mendicott, M., ed. (1992). *Tales for Telling: From Around the World*. New York: Kingfisher Books. Stories from India, China, the Caribbean, Britain, Native Americans, Guyana, Spain.

Minnesota Humanities Commission. (1991). *Braided Lives—An Anthology of Multicultural American Writing*. Minneapolis: Minnesota Council of Teachers of English. Includes over 40 multicultural selections, as well as literature samples by Native Americans, Hispanic Americans, African Americans, and Asian Americans. Recommended for high school and middle school readers.

Navasky, B., ed. and trans. (1993). *Festival in My Heart—Poems by Japanese Children*. New York: Harry N. Abrams. An illustrated collection of poetry by Japanese children printed as a daily feature in Japan's leading newspaper.

Osborne, M.P., ed. (1993). *Mermaid Tales from Around the World* (illustrated by Troy Howell). New York: Scholastic. Includes Celtic and Japanese stories.

Palley, J., ed. (1989). *Best New Chicano Literature 1989*. Tempe, Ariz.: Bilingual Press.

Picard, B.L., ed. (1992). *French Legends, Tales and Fairy Tales*. New York: Oxford University Press.

Tatum, C., ed. (1990). *Mexican American Literature*. San Diego: Harcourt Brace Jovanovich. Includes poems by Pat Moell, prose by Sandra Cisneros, and a short story by Gary Soto.

Terzian, A. (1993). *The Kid's Multicultural Art Book—Art and Craft Experiences from Around the World*. Charlotte, Vt.: Williamson Publishing. Asian, Indian, Hispanic, Guatemalan, and Native American projects include puppets, figurines, plates, and dolls.

Volavkova, H., ed. (trans. by J. Nemcova). (1978). *I Never Saw Another Butterfly—Children's Drawings and Poems from Terezin Concentration Camp, 1942–1944*. New York: Schocken Books. Actual children's poetry and drawings selected from the archives of the State Jewish Museum in Prague.

Wagenhausen, H., ed. (1978). *Cuentos: An Anthology of Short Stories from Puerto Rico*. New York: Schooner Books. Bilingual anthology of twelve short stories by six leading Puerto Rican writers.

Washington, M.H., ed. (1990). *Black-Eyed Susans/Midnight Birds: Stories By and About Black Women*. New York: Anchor Books. Short stories by women writers, including Toni Morrison, Ntozake Shange, Toni Cade Bambana, and Gwendolyn Brooks.

Multicultural Bibliographies

Cohen, D., and M.D. Cohen, eds. (1990). *Resources for Valuing Diversity—The Louis Armstrong Middle School (I.S. 227 Q) Multicultural Collection*. Brooklyn, N.Y.: Board of Education.

Farina, C. (1989). *Making Connections: A K–12 Multicultural Literature Bibliography*. New York: New York City Board of Education. (Address: 110 Livingston Street, Brooklyn, NY 11201)

Horner, C.T. (1981). *The Aging Adult in Children's Books and Non-Print Media*. New York: Scarecrow Press.

Kruse, G., and K. Horning. (1989). *Multicultural Children's, Youth and Adult Literature 1980–1988*. Madison, Wisc.: Cooperative Children's Book Center.

Rudman, M.K. (1984). *Children's Literature: An Issues Approach*. 2nd ed. New York: Longman.

Smallwood, B.A. (1991). *The Literature Connection*. Reading, Mass.: Addison-Wesley. Includes annotated bibliographies of textbooks for foreign speakers, multicultural children's literature, and young adult literature. In addition, it has detailed read-aloud criteria, techniques, and follow-up activities. Read-aloud selections are annotated according to themes and multidisciplinary applications.

Professional Books and Articles for the Multicultural Educator

The following list of references is meant to serve as a starting point for readings in a field where new works are continually being published. As well, the list includes works that I have found helpful in developing classroom activities.

Allport, G.W. (1979). *The Nature of Prejudice*. 25th Anniversary ed. Boston: Addison-Wesley. Classic study of the origins and nature of prejudice.

Baker, G.C. (1994). *Planning and Organizing for Multicultural Instruction*. 2nd ed. Menlo Park, Calif.: Addison-Wesley.

Banks, J.A. (1988). *Multiethnic Education: Theory and Practice*. 2nd ed. Boston: Allyn and Bacon.

Banks, J.A. (1991). *Teaching Strategies for Ethnic Studies*. 5th ed. Boston: Allyn and Bacon. Includes specific multicultural lesson plans and resource lists for various ethnic groups.

Banks, J.A. (December 1991/January 1992). "Multicultural Education: For Freedom's Sake." *Educational Leadership* 49, 4: 32–36.

Banks, J.A. (Fall 1992). "It's Up to Us." (Interview). *Teaching Tolerance*, pp. 20–23.

Banks, J.A., and C. McGee Banks. (1989). *Multicultural Education: Issues and Perspectives*. Boston: Allyn and Bacon.

Bryan, M.B., and B.H. Davis. (1975). *Writing About Literature and Film*. New York: Harcourt Brace Jovanovich.

Council on International Books for Children. (1980). *Winning Justice for All*. New York: Women's Educational Equity Act Program.

Edwards, B. (1989). *Drawing on the Right Side of the Brain*. Los Angeles: Jeremy P. Tarcher.

Gardner, H. (1983). *Frames of Mind*. New York: Basic Books.

Gardner, H. (1991). *The Unschooled Mind*. New York: Basic Books.

Gardner, H. (1993). *Multiple Intelligences*. New York: Basic Books.

Gollnich, D.M., and P.C. Chinn. (1990). *Multicultural Education in a Pluralistic Society*. 3rd ed. Columbus, Ohio: Merrill.

Goodman, K. (1986). *What's Whole in Whole Language?* Portsmouth, N.H.: Heinemann.

Grant, C.A., and C.E. Sleeter. (1989). *Turning on Learning. Five Approaches to Multicultural Teaching*. Columbus, Ohio: Merrill.

Graves, D. (1984). *A Researcher Learns to Write: Selected Articles and Monographs*. Exeter, N.H.: Heinemann Educational Books.

Harvey, J.D. (1992). *Teaching About Native Americans*. Washington, D.C.: National Council for the Social Studies.

Hunter, M. (1984). *Mastery Teaching*. El Segundo, Calif.: T.I.P.

Lockwood, A.T. (Summer 1992). "Education for Freedom." *Focus in Change* 7: 23–29. (National Center for Effective Schools Research & Development).

Nieto, S. (1992). *Affirming Diversity: The Sociopolitical Context of Multicultural Education*. White Plains, N.Y.: Longman.

Olivanes, R.A. (1993). *Using the Newspaper to Teach ESL Learners*. Newark, Del.: International Reading Association.

Pasternak, M.G. (1979). *Helping Kids Learn Multicultural Concepts: A Handbook of Strategies*. New York: Research Press.

Ramsey, P. (1992). *Teaching and Learning in a Di-*

verse World. New York: Teachers College Press, Columbia University.

Ramsey, P.G, E.B. Void, and L.R. Williams. (1984). *Multicultural Education: A Source Book*. New York: Garland.

Reardon, B.A. (1990). *Comprehensive Peace Education*. Colchester, Vt.: Teacher's College Press.

Rosenblatt, L. (1976). *Literature as Exploration*. 3rd ed. New York: Modern Language Association.

Rosenblatt, L. (1978). *The Reader, The Text, The Poem: The Transactional Theory of the Literary Work*. Carbondale: Southern Illinois University Press.

Routman, R. (1991). *Invitations*. Portsmouth, N.H.: Heinemann

Schniedewind, N., and E. Davidson. (1983). *Open Minds and Equality: Sourcebook of Learning Activities to Promote Race, Sex, and Age Equity*. Boston: Allyn and Bacon.

Schuman, J.M. (1980). *Art from Many Hands: Multicultural Art Projects for Home and School*. Englewood Cliffs, N.J.: Prentice Hall.

Sleeter, C., and C.A. Grant. (1988). *Making Choices for Multicultural Education: Five Approaches to Race, Class and Gender*. Riverside, N.J.: Merrill.

Triedt, P.L., and I.M. Triedt. (1990). *Multicultural Teaching: A Handbook of Activities, Information & Resources*. Boston: Allyn and Bacon.

Other Resources: Periodicals, Video, and Centers

Americans All, national education program, provides comparative historical information about six major ethnic groups. Contact: Americans All, One E. Wacker Dr., Ste. 2400, Chicago, IL 60601; (312) 464–9388.

ASCD Curriculum Update, a quarterly newsletter published by the Association for Supervision and Curriculum Development, 1250 N. Pitt St., Alexandria, VA 22314. The September 1993 issue is devoted to multicultural education. For copies (stock no. 611-93149), call ASCD Order Processing, (703) 549-9110.

Multicultural Education, a quarterly magazine published by the National Association for Multicultural Education. $40 per year. Write to: Caddo Gap Press, 3145 Geary Blvd., Ste. 275, San Francisco, CA 94118; (415) 750-9978, Fax (415) 751-0947.

Multicultural Education, a video-based staff development program produced by the Association for Supervision and Curriculum Development, 1250 N. Pitt Street, Alexandria, VA 22314. For ordering information, call ASCD Order Processing at (703) 549-9110; ASCD stock no. 4-94033. A 40-minute videotape shows actual classroom scenes of teachers and students using a multicultural approach to education, in both urban and suburban settings. The video and the 113-page *Facilitator's Guide* (with workshop activities, handouts, and overheads) are based on the theories of James Banks and Carlos Cortés.

REACH Center for Multicultural and Global Education provides cultural awareness training and educational materials that build a positive understanding of cultural diversity. Reach Center, 180 Nickerson St., Ste. 212, Seattle, WA 98109; (206) 284-8584, Fax (206) 285-2073.

Teaching Tolerance, a journal published twice a year by the Southern Law Poverty Center, Montgomery, Alabama. This is a free magazine with articles, teaching strategies, model programs, and resources for teaching multicultural education. Write to: Teaching Tolerance, 400 Washington Ave., Montgomery, AL 36104.

Acknowledgments

The Evolving Multicultural Classroom represents a collection of burgeoning strategies that were developed in partnership with New York City Public School students, parents, and community members over a 20-year period.

Several editors and journals provided an audience for the strategies my students and I had evolved before multiculturalism became a publishing "draw." Among the editors whose encouragement provided me with an audience for and feedback on the multicultural teaching strategies in this book are the following: Philip Anderson, *The NYSEC Monograph* (New York State English Council), who published various versions of the "Fortune Cookies" strategy and the citizenship strategies included in this book; Sharon Thompson and Donna Borst, editors of various *Good Apple* publications; Ben Nelms and Anne Sullivan, *The English Journal*; Charles Suhor and Felice Kaufman, *Notes Plus* (National Council of Teachers of English, NCTE) (see notes accompanying various sections of this book, regarding adaptation of articles published by NCTE); my *Learning Magazine* "professional family" Charlene Gaynor, Jeannette Moss, Lisa Brusman Zaidel, Karen Hansen, Karen Brudnak, Elizabeth Blizzard Whitman, David Hoffman, and Rose Foltz (*Learning* published versions of "Cresting"); Sara Bullard, Jim Carnes, and Elsie Williams, *Teaching Tolerance* (which published a version of the "Leaving Out to Pull In" strategy); Sharon Franklin, *The Writing Notebook*; and Anita Best, *The Computing Teacher*.

Many of the "Newspapers in Education" strategies included here were first developed and shared in workshops for the New York Newsday in Education (NIE) program. Patricia Houk, Barbara Duncan, and Carol Hacker of NIE have fostered presentations of the strategies in this book in their diversity workshops.

The IMPACT II national teacher-to-teacher network supported the programs promoted by the strategies in this book through social issues grants to the "Bill of Responsibilities" project and showcasing of the strategies at workshops. Ellen Dempsey, President; Ellen Meyers, Director of Programs and Communications; Rafael Ortiz, Director of Technical Assistance and Development; and Margo K. Jones, the former Director of New York City Impact II, encouraged the dissemination of *The Evolving Multicultural Classroom* activities throughout the 27-member sites of the network.

Pilot workshops and a course that included much of the material in this book were sponsored by Leslie Agard-Jones and Evelyn Kalibala, Office of Multicultural Education, New York City Public Schools; Judy Geweurz, Community School District (CSD) 25; and J. Raye Harper and Marilyn Grant of the New York City Public Schools New Staff Development program. Dave Trevaskis of Temple University Law Education and Participation (LEAP) sponsored an institute in the strategies of this book in Philadelphia. Stephen Radin, Office of Reimburseable Funded Programs/Office of Instructional Technology (New York City Public Schools), not only recognized the need for a multicultural education, but included the activities and themes of this work in eighteen of his Title VII federally funded projects (which were authored by me). Eileen Riese facilitated the training of bilingual/English-as-a-second-language teachers in program strategies. Rita Brause and Dorothy Feola at Fordham University gave me a chance to share these ideas with preservice education students; and Edward Stern (deceased) and Walter C. Verfenstein supported and encouraged the development of these strategies at Ditmas Junior High School (CSD 20).

Another key editor in the field of multicultural education and project director of Geocurrents (New York City Public Schools), Mark Gura, supported, inspired, and collaborated with me in the development of the "Atlas Cards," "Cultural Collages," "Hero Rites," and "Geocurrents" strategies in this book. He also collaborated in conducting workshops around these strategies.

I thank ASCD associate editor Carolyn Pool for her caring, knowledgeable efforts to prepare this book for publication.

Finally, I would like to thank my dear friends Denise and Ed Levine, who supported, nurtured, and shared my initial efforts in multicultural education.

Rose Reissman
New York City

Index

ASCD Resources on Multicultural Education and Diversity

ASCD Books

How to Respond to Your Culturally Diverse Student Population by Sarah LaBrec Wyman. 1993. 52 pages. Stock# 611-93180. $6.95.

The Middle School—And Beyond by Paul S. George, Chris Stevenson, Julia Thomason, and James Beane. 1992. 166 pages. Stock# 611-92016. $14.95.

Global Education: From Thought to Action. Kenneth Tye, editor. 1991 ASCD Yearbook. 184 pages. Stock# 611-91004. $19.95.

ASCD Networks

Global Education Network. For information, contact Marilyn McKnight, Milwaukee Public Schools, Forest Home School, P.O. Drawer 10K, Milwaukee, WI 53201. Telephone: (414) 645-5200.

Bilingual Education & Other Appropriate Practices for Language Minority Students. For information, contact Rosita Apodaca, Assistant Supt., Dallas Public Schools, 3835 Canot Lane, Dallas, TX 75244. Telephone: (214) 824-1620.

Educational Leadership

Theme issue on educating for diversity. Feature article by and interview with James A. Banks. May 1994 (vol. 51, no. 8). Stock# 1-94050. $5.00; discounts on multiple copies.

Theme issue on multicultural issues, entitled "Whose Culture?" Topics include African-American immersion, multicultural education projects, history, literature, and scientific literacy. Includes an interview with Matthew Prophet. December 1991/January 1992 (vol. 49, no. 4). Stock no. 611-91119. $5.00.

Theme issue on how to deal with diversity issues such as ability, gender, and style differences. Special feature sections on whole language and discipline. March 1989 (vol. 46, no. 6). Stock# 611-89009. $4.00.

Theme issue on the diversity of at-risk students. Topics include restructuring the urban elementary school, dropout prevention, bilingual students, Native American students, and transracially adopted children. February 1989 (vol. 46, no. 5). Stock# 611-89008. $4.00.

Videotape

Multicultural Education. Features James Banks and Carlos Cortés in a 40-minute program that introduces basic principles of multicultural education. Includes a 113-page facilitator's guide and the book *Teaching with a Multicultural Perspective: A Practical Guide* by Leonard Davidman and Patricia T. Davidman (New York: Longman, Inc., 1993). Stock# 4-94033. Purchase: $328 (ASCD members), $398 (nonmembers). Rent for five days: $125; Preview: $20.

Audiotapes

Knowledge Construction, Curriculum Transformation, and Multicultural Education. Presenter: J. Banks. From ASCD's 1994 Annual Conference. Stock# 2-94145. $9.95.

Educating for Cultural Diversity: A Conversation with James Banks. Presenters: J. Banks and R. Brandt. From ASCD's 1994 Annual Conference. Stock# 2-94146. $9.95.

Multicultural Education: A Critical Change Variable in the School System of the 21st Century. Presenter: S. Rawlings. From ASCD's 1994 Annual Conference. Stock# 2-94149. $9.95.

The Influence of Cultural Diversity and the Changing Family on Teaching and Learning in Middle Grades Classrooms. Presenters: E. Sparapani and F. Abel. From ASCD's 1994 Annual Conference. Stock# 2-94-86. $9.95.

Educating for Citizenship in a Multicultural Society. Speaker: M. Turner, Close Up Foundation, Alexandria, Va. 1992. Stock# 612-92091. $9.95.

ASCD Curriculum Update

Theme issue on multicultural education. Editor: John O'Neil. September 1993. 8 pages. Stock# 611-93149. $1.00 per copy; discounts for multiple copies.

Theme issue on global education. Editor: John O'Neil. January 1989. 8 pages. Stock# 611-89014. $1.00 per copy; discounts for multiple copies.

Association for Supervision and Curriculum Development
1250 N. Pitt Street
Alexandria, VA 22314
Phone: (703) 549-9110   Fax: (703) 549-3891